MODERN ART OF CANDLE CREATING

by Don and Ray Olsen

South Brunswick
New York: A.S. Barnes and Company
London: Thomas Yoseloff Ltd

A.S. Barnes and Company., Inc.
Cranbury, New Jersey 08512

Thomas Yoseloff Ltd
108 New Bond Street
London W1Y OQX, England

First Printing 1964
Second Printing 1965
Third Printing 1967
Fourth Printing 1969
Fifth Printing 1970
Sixth Printing 1971

ISBN: 0-498-06280-5

Printed in the United States of America

PUBLISHERS NOTE

Until nine years ago, Ray and Don Olsen, brothers, were tending strictly to their business of providing residential heating equipment to customers in hometown Seattle. Then, one day, their mother, whose hobby was the making of ornamental candles, made a request of Ray.

"Could you make me some metal molds?" she asked, explaining that she was thoroughly dissatisfied with the results obtained with candle molds improvised from such odds and ends as milk and cottage-cheese cartons.

"I think so," said Ray, an experienced sheet-metal worker. He came back several days later with round, square and star-shaped molds. They were just what the doctor ordered. Soon friends of his mother's who had been struggling with haphazard, contrived molds were urging him to make them some fancy molds, too. Like smoke signals, word soon spread around Puget Sound. One thing led to another. The growing number of candle-making hobbyists had difficulties rounding up needed materials: Stearic acid, proper waxes, wicking, candle scent, color rosettes, candle glitter and sequin pins, votive candles and votive-candle glasses. The Olsens found sources and began filling orders. The result was the Pourette Manufacturing Company—one of the largest candle-making supply firms in the United States, and the only company manufacturing metal candle-making molds for home use.

Today on the wall of their modern office in Seattle a pin map shows the localities of dealers throughout the United States, including Alaska and Hawaii, and in British Columbia, Switzerland, Thailand, and West Indies. All told, the Olsens have 150 outlets handling their candle supplies, and the list continues to grow.

Because the candles can be made easily in any home kitchen, the Olsens' molds have made a lot of little businesses possible. One young man, a spastic, in a short time made $300 worth of candles which his mother sold. Religious organizations and clubs, especially Girl Scouts and Camp Fire Girls, have earned money for their projects by learning the art.

The rediscovery of this form of lighting dating back before the time of Christ is rapidly becoming one of the greatest phenomena of our modern way of life. Each year in the past decade the numbers of people enjoying candle-making have soared.

All of the foregoing seems to be good reason for *Modern Art of Candle Creating*. This is the first and only book of its kind available in the world, and its purpose is to make it possible for those who want to spend their free time learning the art of candle making to get the very utmost in enjoyment from this hobby. Nowhere is the subject covered so well; the authors have collected the best of what they know to be in existence so that basic information could be made available between two covers on all of the principal facets of candle creating and decorating.

Don and Ray Olsen, recognized as the top experts in the art, are to be congratulated for a job well done.

ACKNOWLEDGMENT

Grateful acknowledgment is offered to all those good people who assisted in the making of this book: to our parents, Mr. and Mrs. Leonard Olsen, whose interest in candle-making inspired our quest for better candle-making materials and techniques; and to our wives, Joan and L'Norah, who tirelessly gave of their time and energy in giving countless demonstrations of the modern art of candle creating to enthusiastic hobbyists. Thank you all.

Don and Ray Olsen

Readers who are interested in further information are invited to write to the authors at the Pourette Manufacturing Company, 6818 Roosevelt Way Northeast, Seattle 15, Washington.

Table of Contents

Ray and Don Olsen checking over their Pourette display booth at the Century 21 Center, site of Seattle World's Fair

FOREWORD

"Candle—A slender cylindrical body of tallow wax, or other solid fat, containing a wick, burned to furnish light."

—WEBSTER

There was a time in the long ago—before Thomas Edison—when Webster's definition was correct; candles *were* a necessity in the home because of their light-giving benefits. But Time marches on, and in succeeding years their need as a source of light has greatly diminished.

Still, today, the candle has remained very much a part of our home life.

Why?

What has enabled the "old-fashioned" candle to withstand the inroads of Progress?

Why do we continue to use candles to create a cheerful atmosphere in the home?

Boiled down to their essentials, the benefits of candles are two-fold: the soft, gentle glow of candlelight provides pure captivating beauty, and the candle itself lends ornamental quality.

It takes little ingenuity and creative imagination to turn a slab of wax into a picture of beauty and to add to the decor of any occasion. Their symbol of warmth and friendliness is especially suitable during the Christmas season, but they can also be decorated to adapt to any affair—birthday party, Thanksgiving dinner, wedding anniversary, or whatever.

Candle-crafting offers much pleasure to those of you seeking stimulating hobbies. Not only does it challenge your creative instinct and provide many hours of fun and enjoyment with gratifying results, but it is also a decidedly economical pastime.

With the ever-increasing popularity of candle-making as a hobby, we realized that an up-to-date book on the art was drastically needed. Little was available; the professionals had guarded their secrets well. Through our own research campaign we were fortunate to uncover many ancient secrets and develop new creative and decorative ideas. In addition, numerous candle hobbyists throughout America graciously sent us tips and suggestions drawn from their own experiences. After gathering material for eight years, the result is this single source of modern know-how in candle-crafting.

We hope you will enjoy reading it as much as we have enjoyed putting it together.

... DON AND RAY OLSEN

INTRODUCTION

Today's modern candle bears small resemblance to the old-fashioned variety of yesteryear. Webster's definition—"a slender cylindrical body of wax containing wick"—needs broadening. You have only to stroll through a department store candle display and see the heterogeneous selection of bright colors, shapes and styles to fully appreciate the advancement of the art.

Yet, despite all this, the basic production methods have remained the same; they are either molded, dipped or rolled. The "molding" method, of course, remains the more complex of the three in that it involves procuring and preparing a mold, melting and pouring the wax, and preparing the candle for display. It's the most interesting and challenging of the three methods.

The second method—dipping—involves successive dippings of wick in a vat of molten wax until the desired thickness of the candle is reached. This process, however, is not covered in this book because the average hobbyist does not have the equipment necessary to create satisfactory results, nor is the desire to create tapers prevalent with him. Creating tapers is more to the liking of professional candle makers, with their huge wax vats, wick holders and knowledge of wax characteristics so important in producing tapers. Moreover, professional tapers hardly can be improved upon for beauty and cost, so it isn't worthwhile for the hobbyist to undertake this phase. Additionally, tapers, while decorative in themselves, do not lend well to decorating due to their slim diameter. Consequently, there is little incentive for the "kitchen candle makers" to create tapers since the challenge and fun of candle decorating is missing.

Perhaps there will be a few who will disagree with our analysis and will argue that a true candle enthusiast receives pleasure and satisfaction regardless of the method or style used. These venturesome handful notwithstanding, the dipping of tapers will not be covered in this book.

The third method of creating candles—the rolled beeswax fashion—requires very little explanation. As a matter of fact, any store selling sheet beeswax will automatically have instruction booklets available to cover the subject adequately for you.

Therefore, the bulk of this book will be devoted to the *molding* method of candle making. Four broad factors will be thoroughly covered:

Proper material and equipment. Here we will discuss items both necessary and helpful in the actual creating of the candle itself, excluding the decorating aspect.

Up-to-date "know-how." Detailed instructions on casting the four basic types of candles will be revealed.

Creating and decorating techniques. Numerous techniques enabling the novice to begin producing beautifully decorated candles immediately will be completely outlined.

Decorating ideas for all occasions. Contained in this section are many useful ideas for employing candles to enhance the decor of any season, affair or event.

But enough of this preamble.

We know you are anxious to begin learning how to make candles.

So let's go to work.

PART I

PROPER MATERIALS
AND EQUIPMENT
FOR MOLDING CANDLES

Proper Facilities and Equipment

ADEQUATE WORKING AREA

Your own kitchen is perhaps the best working area since you will need water and a stove. Before starting the actual steps of making a candle, and assuming your kitchen will be your work shop, it is advisable to take certain precautions in the preparation of your working area. Here are some rules to remember:

Always spread a newspaper or wrapping paper, along with wax paper, over your working area for protection. Wax drippings which fall upon the wax paper can then be scraped up and remelted in the melting pot. Newspapers are least desirable for this purpose because wax drippings also pick up the newsprint and consequently cannot be reused.

If there is any danger of leakage or breakage of your mold while pouring, confine the mold in a can or similar container to catch any running or seeping wax. Avoid pouring the mold in or near your sink; melted wax and a sink drain do not mix.

Wear a plastic apron while pouring and decorating as wax has a way of splattering occasionally.

MELTING POT

An old coffee can or metal pitcher with a spout is best for melting wax, though a large

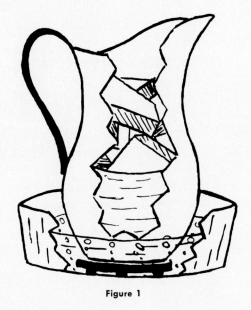

Figure 1

coffee or shortening can is adequate if a spout is squeezed out to facilitate pouring. Should you harbor any doubts about the pouring capabilities of your melting pot, coat the pouring side of the brim with a cold, wet cloth. This will prevent dribbling down the side. And here's another safety hint: While melting the wax it is best to keep the pot in a pan of water with a trivet of some sort set in the pan to permit free water flow under the pot. (See Figure 1.)

If temperatures higher than 190 degrees are desired, the pot can be placed on the

Picture 1

direct heat providing you take the following precautions:

Use a wax with a melting point no lower than 130 degrees.

Wipe exterior of pot clean of any wax film.

Stir the wax occasionally and never leave the pot unattended.

Keep thermometer in the pot; don't allow the temperature to exceed 300 degrees.

In event the molten wax ignites—we've never known this actually to happen but it's wise to be prepared—you can extinguish it by (1) placing a pie tin or similar flat object over the pot to smother the flame, or (2) sprinkling powdered baking soda into the pot. *Never use water to extinguish a wax fire.*

WATER BATH CONTAINER

Professionals cool their candles initially in a water bath, and we strongly recommend that you have one to create smooth, glossy finishes on your candles. The container should be of sufficient depth to allow the mold to be immersed to within three-quarters of an inch from the top of the mold, or to the point of wax level in the mold. Providing the container is deep enough, you can make a water bath out of a water bucket, waste paper basket, kitchen garbage pail, restaurant-sized food cans, etcetera; or you can go to your local sheet metal shop and have an eight-inch-diameter galvanized pipe soldered onto a base.

MOLDS

Two types of molding equipment are normally used by the candle enthusiast—professional, and improvised. Professional equipment is designed specifically for candle making and we'll discuss that first.

PROFESSIONAL MOLDS

The most widely used professional molds today are Pourette metal molds, designed and manufactured strictly for molding candles by both the professional and the hobbyist. Each mold is constructed of heavy durable metal and has the capability of producing an unlimited number of smooth, glossy, truly beautiful candles. (See Photo 1.)

All Pourette molds are slightly tapered, some more than others depending on the shape, to insure simple removal of the candle from the mold which is so important.

IMPROVISED MOLDS

These consist of molds not specifically designed for candle making, yet are nevertheless satisfactory for creating unique, novel candles of various shapes. In this category there is virtually no limit to what can be used: cardboard milk and ice cream containers, plastic containers, cake and pie pans, cookie cutters, muffin tins, cups, jello molds, bowls, plastic or rubber balls, funnels, and so forth. (See Figure 2.) Don't forget, however, that you must slide the solidified wax out of the mold in one piece so that the opening of the mold is its largest part. To assist in proper mold release with improvised molds it is best to grease them with a salad oil or cooking oil just prior to use.

COMBINATION PROFESSIONAL-IMPROVISED MOLDS

This group consists of molds that have been created solely for the purpose of candle making but are actually replicas of small figures not necessarily meant to be used as candles. Contradictory? Maybe this example will clarify that statement for you. Say, for instance, that you have a salt shaker with a peculiar shape and you desire to duplicate the exact shape in the form of a candle. With the aid of liquid rubber, which we will discuss in more detail later, you are able to create a rubber flexible mold, from which an unlimited number of exact replicas can be made. The salt shaker was improvised while the rubber mold became professional; thus you have a combination professional-improvised mold. (See Picture 6.)

Figure 2

Figure 3

MOLD ACCESSORIES

WICK HOLDER

Whenever the wick is secured to a mold before pouring, it must be held by a wick holder. This is merely a "rod" of some sort that lies across the open span of the mold to hold and center the wicking.

Improvised wick holders frequently used with the larger molds are a pencil, darning needle, long nail, stick, and a cut coat hanger. Match sticks and opened paper clips are often used additionally for the smaller molds.

WICK TAB

These small tabs are invaluable when making a container-type candle. Since there is no wick hole at the bottom of this type of mold through which the wick is secured, our Pourette wick tabs are made specifically for the purpose of centering and holding the wick. (See Figure 3.) In an emergency, however, a small button split shot, nut, etcetera, can serve as a substitute.

MOLD SEALER

This remarkable sealer is a reusable "clay-like solder" that adheres tightly and firmly to metal, thereby serving a useful function.

Wherever a wick hole exists through the base of a metal mold, there's the possibility of either wax seeping out or water—if the mold is water-cooled—seeping in. Mold sealer prevents both. (See Figure 4.) To aid in the prevention of seepage, take the following precautionary measures:

Clean the bottom of the mold thoroughly, removing any wax, dirt or film left from Scotch tape or masking tape.

After the wick retainer screw is in place, wad up a piece of sealer so that it resembles a disc, about an inch in diameter, and press it tightly over the screw, forming a seal.

The mold can now be poured. If, after use, the sealer becomes impregnated with particles of wax, simply drop the "wad" in boiling water until the wax separates from the sealer and floats to the surface.

If you are without mold sealer when ready to pour, then ordinary masking tape (available at any hardware store) is a good substitute. It won't guarantee as air-tight a seal as regular mold sealer, but it generally eliminates seepage if applied liberally.

MISCELLANEOUS EQUIPMENT

THERMOMETER

The temperature of the wax is vital when pouring a candle, and, therefore, a reliable

Figure 4

thermometer is essential in the production of top-quality candles. We recommend a regular cooking thermometer, with a glass-encased scale ranging up to 300 degrees. This convenient pan-clip type enables the thermometer to remain immersed in the molten wax until the desired temperature is attained.

WICK RETAINER SCREW

This is required only when using a metal mold containing a wick hole through which the wick is inserted. The wick retainer screw secures the wick tightly, helping seal the wick hole and preventing wax seepage. If the wick hole is normal size (⅛" diameter), No. 6⅜" tapping screw is recommended.

Molding Equipment: Proper Care

CARE OF YOUR MOLD

If and when you invest in a professional mold you'll naturally want to keep it in perfect condition for as long as possible. Consequently, your mold will have to be treated with the same loving care as a fine precision tool, with particular precautions taken not to mar or contaminate the inside. Any scratches or dents, dust or foreign matter in your mold will affect the candle's surface.

RULES TO REMEMBER

To get the most out of your mold, abide by the following rules:

Never strike it with a hard object.

Never place it in an oven with a temperature exceeding 175 degrees.

Never scratch the interior with a sharp instrument or abrasive.

Never loan to friends unless they know how to care for it.

Store in a warm, dry place to prevent rust; keep covered to protect interior from dust.

If you should find it necessary to clean your mold of contaminated or "stubborn wax," use one of these methods:

Easy Method. Pour your next candle with the wax at 230 degrees. This usually cleans the mold and absorbs stubborn wax.

Oven Method. Place the mold on its side in a cookie pan lined with aluminum foil and put into a *preheated* oven of 175 degrees or less. Keep the assembly away from hot coils by placing it on the rack midway in the oven. After fifteen minutes, any wax in the mold should be drained onto the foil.

Chlorothene Method. First, place mold sealer or masking tape over the wick hole. Next, pour one-half cut of Chlorothene into the mold. Now hold pad over opening of the mold and swirl the solution around the interior. Then wrap a soft rag around the end of a stick and rub the mold until all stubborn wax has been removed. Last, pour the solution from the mold and allow the mold to dry thoroughly before using again.

A brisk treatment with Silicon Spray is sometimes used for double assurance of proper mold release *after* the mold has been fully cleaned.

CARE OF PANS AND UTENSILS

If you've been using a double boiler to melt wax, you will probably want to clean it afterwards. To accomplish this simply melt and pour off excess wax, wipe clean with a paper towel, and wash in hot, soapy water.

Smaller utensils can be cleaned in the same manner, or by putting them into a pan of boiling water. The wax will melt off the utensils; being lighter than water, it will rise to the surface and form a film. Let the water cool, then remove the hardened wax film and retrieve your utensils.

CLOTHING CARE

Clothing might not be considered a part of actual molding equipment, but suggestions as to how garments can be cleaned of splattered wax are certainly worth knowing.

Unwashable Clothing. Pick off as much of the wax as possible and send it out to a professional dry cleaner.

Washable Clothing. After picking off as much wax as possible, place the cloth between paper towels and press with an iron at moderate temperature. Possibly the material will have to be washed several times before the wax stain is totally removed.

Let us stress once more, however, that you can avoid having to clean your clothing of wax if you will wear a plastic apron or covering of some sort when working with wax.

Molding Materials

WAX

Early Americans made candles from tallow or beeswax, but nowadays those ancient ingredients have been replaced with high-temperature refined paraffin wax. Tallow's smoking characteristics and obnoxious odor render it unsatisfactory, while the high cost of beeswax candles, though beautiful and adequate, prohibit the average hobbyist from using it.

With the advent of paraffin wax, in 1850, a big step was made in candle making. It was discovered that paraffin candles give more light per unit, burn without any odor, and leave no ash. It was quickly noted, however, that the lower melting point paraffin (approximately 120°) was inadequate for successful candle making for several reasons:

They lost their shape in hot weather, melted too rapidly and dripped excessively, thereby necessitating the addition of a hardening substance such as stearic acid or beeswax. Today, however, high temperature paraffin waxes are available, making it possible to create candles without the use of a hardening substance. These higher temperature waxes range from 125° to 160° melting point, thereby offering the candle hobbyist a wide range.

Most superior petroleum waxes within this range, regardless of their manufacturer, are capable of producing very beautiful, sturdy candles. No single type of wax fills all the needs of every type of candle, however. The type of wax you select (if you have a choice)

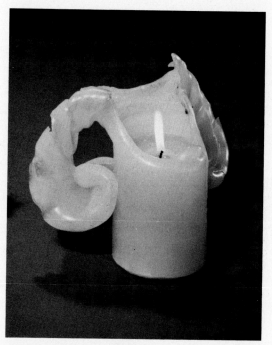

Picture 3

should depend on the type of candle you are creating (block, container, novelty, etc.) and the characteristics you wish to acquire (translucent or opaque, mottled or clear, etc.).

A further factor to consider in choosing your wax is whether the wax is prone to *splay* (some refer to it as *foliate*) as it burns. This is to have the excess wax on the edges curl outwards rather than drip, as is normally desired in the large block candle because of its graceful appearance. (See Picture 3.)

	WAXES			WAX ADDITIVES	
	Melt. Temp. 125-130°	Melt. Temp. 143-160°	Bees- wax	Lustre Crystals	Stearic Acid
Glossy finish	X	X		X	
Good mold release	X	X		X	X
Longer burning			X	X	X
Translucent	X	X			
Opacity			X	X	X
Prone to splay	X				
Prone to melt out to brim	X				
Prone to burn down interior			X	X	X
Soft and pliable for hand molding			X		
More draft resistant	X		X	X	X
Tends to mottle (add oil or scent to wax)					
May mottle	X	X			
Won't mottle			X	X	X

Actually, with softer waxes (125°-135°) this splaying action is unavoidable if left burning for any length of time, because such waxes are more prone to bend outward at temperatures too high for the wax to be rigid and too low for it to melt. Harder waxes are not as susceptible to bending with temperature increases and are less apt to splay.

A further word should be added about the length of continuous burning time; this has a direct effect on the extent of foliation. To encourage foliation, regardless of the wax used, the candle should burn at least four hours continuously to allow the wax around the edge to soften enough to bend outward.

Before purchasing your wax or adding any of the wax additives, consider the above check list for the performance properties of Pourette waxes.

From this schedule it is obvious that certain waxes are preferable for creating certain candles. For instance, a superior block candle requires a refined wax with a melting point of 143° to 150°; for a container candle, use a wax with a melting point of 125° to 130°; for a candle you must mold by hand, use beeswax.

Remnants of store-bought candles or your own are perfectly suitable for using again to fashion new candles. If they are exceptionally dirty, scrape them clean before melting, but it isn't necessary to first remove the old wick. The wick settles to the bottom of the pan as the wax melts and can be picked out after the new candle has been poured.

WAX ADDITIVES

Stearic Acid. The discovery of this fatty acid has proven to be a major asset to the candle industry. The addition of stearic acid to paraffin does not raise the melting point of the wax but does improve the burning quality and makes a stronger and harder candle. Stearic acid itself forms a hard crystal which forms a matrix within the candle, furnishing a resistant framework. By making the candle harder and stronger, the candle also becomes longer burning. In addition, stearic acid tends to make the candle more opaque.

The amount to be added to paraffin depends upon the initial melting temperature of the paraffin and the desired melting point of the mixture. A tested formula, using low melting paraffin (120°), is to combine one part stearic acid with two parts paraffin. When used with a high temperature paraffin (135° to 150°), approximately three tablespoons to one pound of wax will upgrade the quality of the candle considerably.

Lustre Crystals. This synthetic material, now available at most candle making supply stores, is one of the "secret" ingredients used by professionals to enhance the beauty and quality of candles. Due to their high melting point, these crystals, like stearic acid, not only make the candle harder, longer burning and opaque—but they do more. A level teaspoon per two pounds of wax will produce a small flame; hence, less smoking. This also provides the candle with a hard, glossy surface. If no coloring is added to the wax, the presence of these crystals produces a chalk-white appearance. This "whitening" tendency makes it possible to create exceedingly beautiful wedding or anniversary candles.

Beeswax. We are speaking here of the bulk beeswax, not the beeswax sheets used for rolling candles. This wax is the substance which is secreted by honeybees, from which they make the cells of their comb. It is one of the highest quality waxes available because of its high melting point, superior all around quality, and the rich appearance it renders. Because of this, beeswax candles are generally used as altar candles in churches.

Beeswax is normally not used by hobbyists, and the reasons for that are three-fold: It is hard to come by, is very expensive, and its "tacky" characteristic hinders proper mold release. Should you be fortunate enough, however, to have a substantial supply of beeswax available, there are ways in which it can be used successfully. One way—particularly for the hobbyist who can procure only low temperature paraffin—is to blend the beeswax with the paraffin. The following two formulas have proven invaluable in upgrading the quality of the finished candle:

Paraffin 50%
Beeswax 50%
Paraffin 70%
Beeswax 10%
Stearic Acid 20%

An alternate way of utilizing a supply of beeswax is the double-pouring technique. Fill your mold with regular wax, place it in a water bath, and let it "set up" for approximately ten minutes. Then pour out the liquid wax in the center and refill the mold with the liquid beeswax. By using your beeswax in this manner, you are taking advantage of its superior burning quality, yet are not hindered by its poor mold release quality.

WICK

Perhaps no other item means so much to successful candle making as the wick. The supplier from whom you purchase your

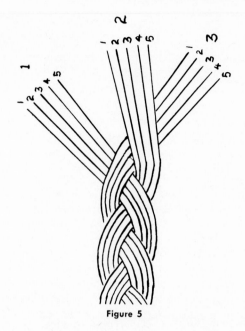

Figure 5

wick should be able to advise you as to the proper size, but a little knowledge about its characteristics is very worthwhile.

Wicking made of cotton yarn and treated for proper burning is normally plaited, square-braided, or with a wire center. Understanding the three types of wicking is necessary for those who wish to create candles that burn properly.

TYPES OF WICK

Flat-braided or plaited three-strand wick. The most common type, it is used for the larger block candles and is identified by the total number of threads of yarn making up the wick. For example: 15-ply wick contains 15 threads, five threads in each of the three strands. (See Figure 5.) This wick has a 90° bend while burning, allowing the tip to extend outside the flame, where it is reduced to a glowing ash and dissipated in the air. With good stock (that which has been scoured and boiled to remove any oils in the cotton) there should be no accumulation of carbon or ash.

Square-braided wick. Due to its compact structure, this wick is more self-supporting than the flat-braided; ideal for candles with relatively small diameters. The reason is obvious. The smaller the candle's diameter, the less wax it has to melt and consume horizontally. Therefore, it burns at a greater rate. The wick, however, may not burn at such a rate unless it is sturdy enough to remain erect in the flame, where it can be consumed. The square-braided wick meets this requirement, whereas the flat-braided tends to flop over and impair the proper burning of the candle.

This type of bleached wick guarantees the removal of any impurities.

Metal core wick. Where a candle is contained in a vessel and there is liquid wax surrounding it, the metal core supports the wick so that it stands straight. The wire in the wick melts as the candle burns and, since this wick does not bend, carbon accumulates. No harm is caused, however, should it fall into the molten wax. Because of its rigidity, metal core wick is much easier to work with when pouring a container type candle.

Small wire wick which gives off a small flame is often used in making taper candles to make them drip, if dripping is desired.

When using this type of wick, remember the end should be waxed before lighting the first time to facilitate burning.

SIZES OF WICK

It has been shown that the type of candle to be created determines the type of wick to be used. The next step is to select the correct size of wick which is directly related to the diameter of the proposed candle. Other factors, such as wax hardness, cost, and purpose of the candle, also are to be considered, but since most of us use a high temperature paraffin wax and prefer a normal long-burning candle that drips as little as possible, the diameter remains the key factor. The following fundamentals explain the relationship between the wick, the flame, and the candle diameter:

When the wick is first lit the flame feeds on the wick alone. As the candle burns, the flame melts the surrounding wax which, because of its viscosity, is absorbed by the wick and ultimately consumed by the flame. The heat of the now well-fed flame continues to melt additional wax and the process continues. With a tapered candle, the small candle diameter limits the amount of wax melted by the flame and the wick has little trouble absorbing that which has melted. Therefore, little or no dripping will result since there is no excess melted wax to broach the sides of the candle. In some instances such as small diameter candles, the wick is too large and absorbs the melted wax faster than it can be accumulated, causing the flame to smoke. Incidentally, in a strong draft, any candle will smoke and drip unless the candle diameter is exceedingly large.

The situation is quite different in large block candles where the sides are relatively far removed from the flame. In this case, the flame will melt wax, predominantly in the horizontal direction, faster than it can burn. Consequently, a large pool of wax is formed; how this pool performs is important. If the wick is too small to absorb the melted wax, as is often the case in larger candles, the sides of the candle will broach, causing an overflow or drip. As the wax overflows and runs down the sides, the wick will smoke momentarily until a fresh supply of melted wax is available for the wick to consume. Should the wick be too small, the flame will tend to sink into the body of the candle, leaving a wax-shell around the edges.

Essentially, a properly burning wick is one that consumes the melted wax as rapidly as it accumulates. You will observe that in a good dripless candle the cup is almost dry. With the exception of where the wick is too small and the flame sinks into the center of the candle, it can be stated that if the wick is too large, the candle will smoke; if too small, the candle will drip (See Figure 6.)

Though we recognize the reasons causing a candle to drip, it is difficult to create a dripless candle larger than 1¼" in diameter.

This is due to the fact that normal wicking available is not large enough to absorb the liquid wax in a candle this size or larger.

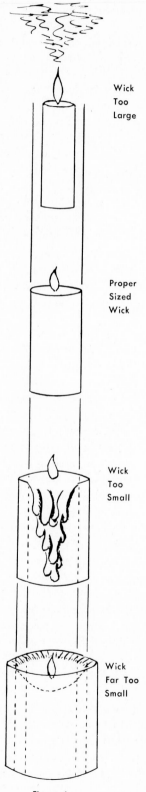

Wick
Too
Large

Proper
Sized
Wick

Wick
Too
Small

Wick
Far Too
Small

Figure 6

Since most candles range in size from ½″ to 4″, we have conducted experiments to determine the proper type and size wick to use with candles within this range. The following scale is the result of our findings:

Diameter—Proper Wick

Common type under 2″—#1/0 bleached square wick

Common type over 2″—30-ply unbleached flat braided wick

Container type under 2″—small wire core wick #34-40

Container type over 2″—large wire core wick #44-20-18

If you cannot locate regular wicking or need to improvise some in a hurry, you can substitute the following material and formula: Soak cotton yarn for eight hours in a solution of two tablespoons of borax, one tablespoon salt, and one cup of water.

COLOR

Wax may be colored by using only oil-soluble colors. Water-soluble colors such as cake or fruit coloring will not mix with the wax. Coloring "buds" or "sticks" made specifically for coloring wax are far superior to such substitutes as oil paints, color crayons, lipstick, etc. Oil paints are very costly and take a long time to mix with the wax, necessitating continual stirring. Diluting an oil paint with coal oil will solve the mixing problem but presents a new one. Handling coal oil, with its low flash point, is quite dangerous around a hot burner and hot wax.

Some wax crayons such as those distributed by the Glow Candle Co. are very good, for they were made specifically for coloring candles. Others, however, are impregnated with preservatives and dyes that will not be consumed by the wick, causing the flame to sputter, smoke and finally die out altogether. In addition, coloring from most crayons has a tendency to settle in molten wax, thereby leaving the finished candle with a varying shade of color. Lipstick has the same deficiencies as crayons.

Regular wax dye or coloring assures even

coloring throughout the wax, leaves no sediment and does not affect the proper burning of the wick. These dyes may be in the form of either small rosettes or stick and are added to the wax by shaving off small portions or swishing the dye through the wax until the desired color is obtained. Most available coloring buds are very concentrated and capable of coloring at least eight pounds of wax. Lighter or darker shades may be acquired simply by adding more or less of the "bud." For example, pink may be acquired by using a very small amount of the red bud.

SCENT

Scented candles were mentioned many times in the Bible and there is evidence from ancient Egyptian literature and records that the Pharaohs repeatedly burned candles with sweet fragrances.

In scenting any candle, it must be remembered that only an oil base scent will be effective. Most perfumes having either an alcohol or water base are not compatible with wax. In other words, ordinary commercial perfumes, colognes, incense, etc., are completely consumed by the flame and dissipate with no aroma. Oil-base scents not only have pleasant smells but continue to emit their scent while the candle burns. It is best to place scented candles in the lowest spot possible to allow scented vapors to rise. Do not place in a spot where a draft will carry the fragrance away.

Scented candles have a variety of uses in the home. A sweet-smelling scent such as pine, bayberry or rose adds enchantment to any room. Scents with disinfectant properties —sulphur, iodine, citronella—help keep away bothersome insects. Any of the sweet scents help overcome unpleasant cooking odors, and when burned in a sickroom their fragrance is most welcome and beneficial.

There are several ways in which scent can be added to the candle, but the most popular and effective method is to add the scent to the melted wax just prior to pouring the mold (See Figure 8-A). A quarter-ounce of pure undiluted oil scent is sufficient to scent two or three pounds of wax. Other methods frequently used are: (1) dip the wick in scent before securing it to the mold; (2) pour the scent into the cavity of the candle at the same time the "well" is refilled (See Figure 8-B); (3) add the scent to the base of the wick while the candle is burning.

If the scent is added to the wax prior to pouring the mold, be careful not to add an excess amount, for an over-abundance of any oil in wax will cause mottling within the candle.

Figure 8-A

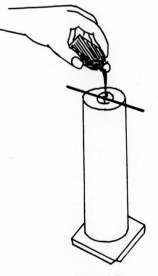

Figure 8-B

PART II

POURING THE CANDLE:
PHASES OF

Securing the Wick: Methods

In reviewing what already has been written, we have tried to emphasize that you can't use just "any old wick" and expect the candle to burn properly. So assuming you have taken special pains to select the correct wick, you must now get this wick into the wax to form a candle.

Two requirements must be kept in consideration when applying wick. First, the wick must be centered in the candle, and, secondly, it must extend far enough inside the candle to assure maximum burning time.

The method used in most cases is determined by the type of mold, but when you are given a choice of more than one method, the final selection is merely a matter of personal preference. All told, the various techniques can be broken down into two broad groups: (A) Securing the wick *before* casting (pouring), and (B) securing the wick *after* casting.

METHODS OF SECURING WICK BEFORE CASTING

WITH METAL MOLDS CONTAINING WICK HOLE

This group includes both professional and improvised metal molds. With the former the hole already is there, while the latter necessitates drilling a hole with an eighth-inch bit.

Pourette molds fall into this category and the instructions accompanying each mold outline the following procedure:

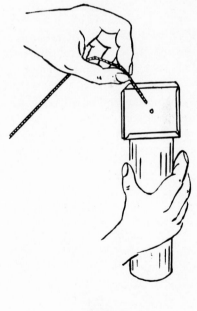

Figure 9

Insert the wick (uncut) from the underside of the mold and thread it through the hole until it reaches the top of the mold. (See Figure 9.) Secure the wick at the top to the wick holder, which lies across the mold opening (See Figure 10). Here several methods may be employed to secure the wick to the wick holder, such as actually tying it, clamping it on with a clothes pin, or securing it with masking tape.

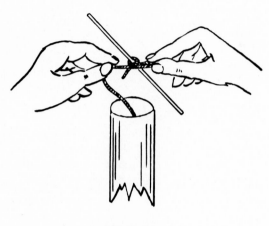

Figure 10

Now, with the wick tightly secured at the mold opening, pull it taut at the point of insertion (base of the mold) and secure with the retainer screw.

Finally, wind the end of the wick counterclockwise under the head of the screw and cut it roughly an inch away (See Figure 11).

Figure 11

Tighten the screw and secure with either mold sealer or masking tape to prevent seepage. The mold is now ready for pouring (See Figure 12).

With improvised metal molds (tin cans, jello molds, metal drinking glasses, etc.) you can employ this same technique, though you will have to drill your own hole in the base. By doing this, your improvised mold becomes a semi-professional mold, for now it can't be used for anything but candle making.

One type of improvised mold with a hole already at the base is the common household funnel. Of course, the "wick hole" is far too large and must be sealed with either mold sealer or a modeling clay after the wick is inserted. You may even fill this hole with a wad of wet paper, but then the wick also

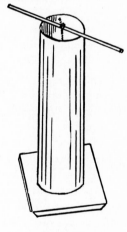

Figure 12

becomes wet, necessitating a drying out period before the finished candle becomes useable. Place the funnel in a glass to hold it upright when pouring in the wax.

MOLD SEALER METHOD

Assuming you don't want a hole drilled in your jello mold or drinking cup, or you are using a glass or plastic mold in which you can't readily drill a hole, then this method offers the solution. The steps are simple:

Press a small wad of mold sealer over

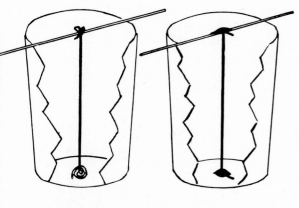

Figure 13   Figure 14

Determine the proper length of wick and secure one end to a wick tab, split shot, button or similar small object. When using lead core wick, it is advisable to cut the wick so that the weighted end swings free about ¼″ above the bottom of the container. This is to allow for expansion and lengthening of the wick when subjected to the heat of the wax; thus, preventing the wick from "bowing" off center if the weighted end were touching bottom at the outset.

Tie or clamp the other end to a wick-holder.

Insert the weighted wick into the mold—centering it with the wick holder resting on the mold edge (See Figure 15).

the end of the wick and against the inside base of the mold, thus securing the wick to the bottom (See Figure 13).

After a few turns around the wick-holder with the other end, apply a little mold sealer here to hold it taut.

After the wax has been poured and allowed to harden, withdraw the wax, remove the mold sealer exposing the wick—and that's all there is to it.

COILED WICK METHOD

This method eliminates the necessity of drilling a wick hole through the base, but is only possible when using lead core wick.

Form a small tight coil at one end of the wick and lower it into the mold, positioning the coil so that the wick rises from the center (See Figure 14).

Secure the top of the wick to the wick-holder by giving it a few turns around the holder.

After the wax has been poured, cooled ·and withdrawn, unwind the coil, trim off the excess wick, and your candle is ready to go.

WEIGHTED WICK METHOD

This method also permits insertion of the wick prior to casting, but instead of securing the wick at the base through a wick hole, the wick is weighted down.

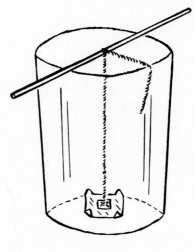

Figure 15

WITH PAPER OR CARDBOARD MOLDS CONTAINING WICK HOLE

Many candle hobbyists use milk cartons, dixie cups, paper cones and cottage cheese cartons for molds and normally secure the wick in much the same manner as with the metal molds. There are a few variations, however, so it is worth covering this group with a separate set of instructions.

Let's use a cottage cheese container as an example.

Cut two small notches at the top edge of the carton on opposite sides.

Poke a small hole in the bottom center of the carton with an ice pick and insert the wick (See Figure 16).

Tie a knot at the loose end to prevent wax seepage through the wick hole.

Pull the wick up until the knot is held firmly against the wick hole.

Lay a wick holder across the top of the carton so it will lie in the two notches previously cut out (See Figure 17).

Drape the upper portion of the wick across the wick holder and secure the loose end to the side of the carton with a rubber band encircling the carton (See Figure 18).

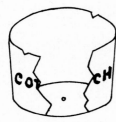

Figure 16

Figure 17

Figure 18

METHODS OF SECURING THE WICK AFTER CASTING

WEIGHTED WICK METHOD

This technique is identical to the weighted wick method previously described, except in this case the wick is lowered into the mold *after* the wax has been poured. Many prefer doing it this way rather than inserting the wick prior to pouring, because it eliminates the problem of trying to pour while attempting to keep the wick from moving off center. This method is very popular in creating container-type candles because the metal core wick remains rigid while being lowered into the liquid wax.

HOLE DRILLED IN WAX METHOD

This method is extremely simple. The wick is merely inserted into the candle after being removed from the mold, with no care needed to weight or secure the wick to the bottom.

Prepare the wick first by dipping it in wax and letting it cool, giving it the rigidity needed for inserting it into the hole.

Drill a hole as far down into the candle as possible (See Figure 19).

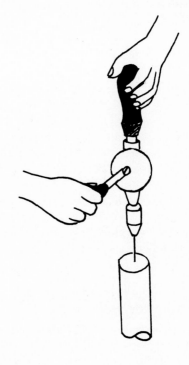

Figure 19

Insert the wick and seal it by pushing a hot metal rod, such as a straight piece of wire cut from a coat hanger, down beside the wick. If the hole is much larger than the wick, merely fill the hole with wax.

HEATED ICE PICK METHOD

If you don't have a drill handy, the wick hole in the candle may be made easily by forcing a heated ice pick or other metal rod into the wax *while it is still soft.* Leave the rod in the candle and pull it out later after the wax has completely hardened.

CHEAP CANDLE METHOD

After the wax has set in the mold long enough for a hardening "crust" to form across the top, poke a hole through this layer to the liquid wax beneath. Then insert

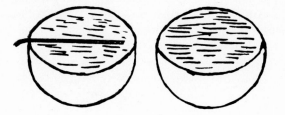

Figure 22

a cheap candle of any kind into the mold so that it protrudes through and is held in position by the hardened wax crust.

TWO-PIECE MOLD METHOD

When two halves are joined together, such as in the case of a snowball candle, the wick can be inserted before the two halves are joined. Mary Pruden, of Riverdale, New Jersey, offers us her version of this technique:

With an ice pick or knife tip, gouge a groove for the wick across the center of one half.

Cut the wick about ½″ longer than the groove, dip in hot wax and lay in place, skipping ½″ at the bottom of the candle. This leaves 1″ of wick at the top, enough so it won't be buried in "snow" if you should later apply whipped wax to the exterior (See Figure 22).

Prepare the two halves for joining by pressing the half without the wick onto a heated cookie tin or pie tin. This softens the wax and permits fusion of the two halves (See Figure 23).

Cement the two halves together with hot wax, making sure there are no air bubbles in the wick groove or center of the candle.

To reinforce the fusion, melt a small amount of wax, pour it into a cookie tin or pie tin, and swirl the seam through this liquid wax (See Figure 24).

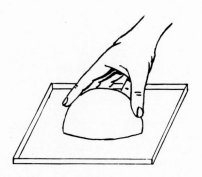

Figure 23

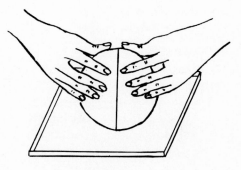

Figure 24

Four Basic Candles: Pouring

BLOCK CANDLES

Block candles are generally considered to be any large decorative candle ranging in diameter from one inch and up. Basic shapes are square, round, and star. Other shapes, however, have been developed, such as oval, hexagon, and triangular. Candles in this category are usually made from a professional mold. Still, some block candles are produced simply by using milk cartons, mailing tubes and so forth as improvised molds.

PROFESSIONAL MOLDS

The following instructions have been patterned after our Pourette mold, but can also be applied to similar molds:

First, insert the wick.

Next, when the temperature of the wax reaches 190 degrees, remove the pot from the flame, wipe excess moisture off to prevent water driplets from entering the candle mold, and slowly pour wax into the mold. Tilt the mold slightly while pouring to prevent the wax from cascading into the mold and causing air bubbles (See Figure 25).

After the candle reaches the desired height, save a cup of wax from this original pouring to fill the well that forms at the top of the mold after the hardening wax has shrunk and settled.

With the mold now filled with liquid wax, allow it to set for about thirty seconds before placing it into the water bath container. The half-minute delay permits all air bubbles to rise to the surface and escape, rather than trapping them inside the mold and pitting the candle's surface.

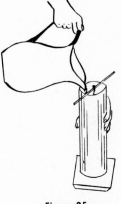

Figure 25

The water should be about bath temperature at immersion. In placing the mold into the water bath, be extremely careful to keep water out of the mold (See Figure 26). Let

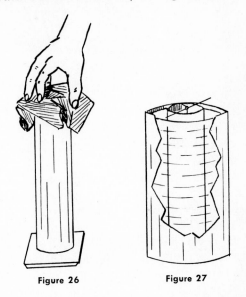

Figure 26   **Figure 27**

the mold remain in the water—weighted down with a heavy object if necessary—during the *setting up* period of approximately two hours (See Figure 27).

About forty-five minutes after the mold is placed in the water, note the wax settling around the wick, forming a deepening well. Now, near the wick, insert a long stick several times through the wax. This will relieve the "surface tension" caused by settling wax, and provide access to the cavities inside the candle. Don't plunge the stick in too fast or you'll be squirted with liquid wax (See Figure 28).

Refill the well and interior cavities with the excess wax you have been saving, being extra careful not to overfill the well. As a matter of fact, refill it only to a point one-quarter inch from the top. The protruding one-quarter inch wall can be easily trimmed off after the candle is withdrawn. The danger of pouring too much wax into the well is that the overflow often seeps between the mold and the hardening wax, making it difficult to remove the finished candle from the mold.

As the wax continues to cool, it will go on contracting and settling, necessitating a *poking* and *refilling* around the wick a couple of times. Allow approximately forty-five minutes between each pouring. You can remove the mold from the water bath any time after the second refill. It can be cooled either at room temperature or in the refrigerator.

If cooled at room temperature, keep the mold off the floor away from cold drafts; allow about eight hours from the initial pouring before removing the candle.

The cooling process can be speeded up considerably via refrigeration, but several precautions must be taken to assure an even cooling process and to prevent *thermal shock* cracks in your candle.

If you use the refrigerator, reverse the position of the mold every half hour. This exposes the colder temperatures at the bottom of the refrigerator to all parts of the wax evenly, instead of limiting it to only the smallest section at the base. Another rule to remember, never leave the mold in the refrigerator after it feels cold to the touch. The wax is ready to be withdrawn at this stage; any overexposure to coldness will result in unsightly cracks around the wax surface. For the same reason, *never* put a mold into a deep freeze.

Not until the mold is cold should any attempt be made to remove the candle. To extract the candle, first remove the retaining

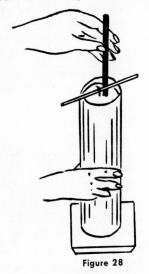

Figure 28

screw, allowing the wick to hang free; remove the wick-holder, turn mold upside
down, tap gently and squarely (if necessary) on a hard surface, and it should drop
right out (See Figure 29). More often than
not, tapping is not necessary.

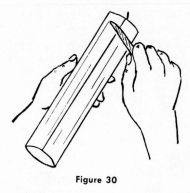

Figure 30

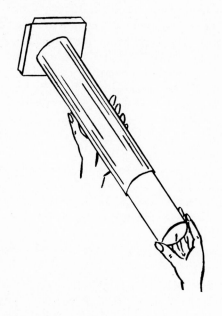

Figure 29

If the mold feels cold but does not release, place it in the refrigerator for about
an hour and then try again. If you are still
unable to remove it, then, *as a last resort,*
pour hot water over the mold. This softens
the wax and normally ruins the candle, but
it does permit withdrawal of the wax.
NEVER BEAT OR PRY on the mold to
remove the wax. Any indenture on the mold
will only tend to hold the wax more firmly,
which adds to your troubles and makes your
mold unsatisfactory for future pourings.

To remove any *seam marks* on the candle
surface accompanying the round cylindrical
molds, take a knife or spatula, hold it out to
the candle at a right angle, and slide it down
the seam (See Figure 30).

For the candle to stand straight, you will
possibly have to square off the base by one
of two methods: Cut and trim with a knife,
or rotate the candle on a heated pie tin,

thereby melting off the irregularities and
smoothing off the base.

After a dark-colored candle has been
poured and in the event you wish to pour a
lighter-colored candle from the same mold,
pour the hot wax down the seam of the
mold as you fill it. This will absorb any bits
of dark wax that might have lodged in the
seam from the previous pouring.

MILK OR SIMILAR CARTONS

Many attractive candles have been produced using milk, cottage cheese, and ice
cream cartons for molds. There are naturally
some disadvantages using any paper or cardboard molds; chiefly the extra work involved
to achieve nice-looking candles. In the case
of the paper or cardboard mold, it is impossible to obtain a sheen to your finished
candle, but this can be partially offset if
you glaze the candle or apply whipped wax
to cover surface blemishes. Both processes
are covered in a later chapter.

The main thing to keep in mind when you
are working with a milk carton or any similar
waxed cardboard container is it is just that
—merely a waxed cardboard container unable to withstand extreme heat or strain.
Take extra precautions in case of wax
leakage or steam bursting. In other words,
SAFETY FIRST, and you won't have a thing
to worry about. We advise these simple
directions for maximum safety and success.

Prepare the milk carton for pouring. Cut
off the top cover with a sharp knife or razor
blade. Wrap masking tape around the top,
middle and bottom, thereby providing added

support to the carton and reducing the risk of seam splitting. The tape encircling the middle also diminishes the "middle aged spread," or bulge, so prevalent with milk cartons.

Secure the wick prior to pouring with the method prescribed for any cardboard mold.

The open tops of milk cartons tend to become diamond-shaped as the wax hardens. This may be prevented by fitting two small sticks of equal length snugly inside the carton near the top between the diagonally opposite corners (See Figure 31).

Figure 31

Place the carton in a bucket or similar container filled with crushed ice or with ½" of cold water on the bottom. The reasoning here is that should any wax seep out, it will be confined within the container. If ice is used, the cooling rate of the wax is accelerated; hence, the period during which the wax exerts its greatest pressure on the walls of the carton is reduced. Consequently, there is less chance of a seam splitting or a noticeable bulge at the sides. If, instead of crushed ice, a ½" of water is used, the danger of wax leakage through the wick hole is eliminated.

Never pour very hot wax in a cardboard container. After the wax has melted in your pot, let it cool until the temperature is approximately 160° before you pour it into the mold. While pouring, be sure to save a small amount of wax with which to refill the well and cavities within the candle.

When completely cold, tear off the carton and you have a square candle—imperfect, but having many possibilities for decorating.

MAILING TUBES OR ANY TUBE OPEN AT BOTH ENDS

Though each end is open, these tubes may still be used to form tall, cylindrical candles if a simple base is added. The base may be either constructed of cardboard or created of wax.

Cardboard base: Cut out a cardboard disc the size of the tube opening and secure it with masking tape. Make sure no holes or cracks are left through which wax may seep out. Swab the tube interior thoroughly with either peanut oil or salad oil to permit a better release and smoother surface on the candle. After the base is attached, insert the wick as previously prescribed. Again, as with the milk carton, pour the wax at approximately 160°. To avoid any possible disaster while pouring, it is advisable to pour the wax while the tube is propped up in a bucket filled with crushed ice. This speeds the cooling process and retards any possible wax leakage.

Wax base: Pour ¼" of wax in a small plate. Set the tube into the puddle of wax and allow it to harden before filling the tube with wax. With this method, the wick must, of course, be applied by the weighted wick method or inserted after the wax has hardened with the heated ice pick or drill method.

TIN CANS

Unlike professional molds, the vast majority of tin cans are not tapered. Consequently, they present a mold release problem. However, they have been most successful in cases where care in choosing the "right" tin can was taken. Any can with a deep "bead" at the base or indentation around the sides will not release the hardened wax. Here are the steps we recommend with a tin can mold:

Grease it first with peanut, olive or salad oil.

Insert the wick using either the "hole-in-base" method or "weighted wick" method.

Pour the mold as you would a professional metal mold.

When you are confident the wax has completely cooled and is ready to withdraw, take a can opener and cut out the bottom of the can. This enables you to *push* the candle out much easier than trying to *pull* it out with the wick.

We know of one candle hobbyist who did everything as we have just outlined, but she could only force the candle out about halfway. Rather than get frustrated and "chucking" the whole thing out, she left the candle half in the can, sprayed and decorated both the can and candle, and came up with a candle and built-in base that looked remarkably attractive.

NOVELTY CANDLES

A *novelty candle* has an unusual shape and gives the appearance of being something other than a candle. These candles are normally smaller than block candles and are created from two-piece molds, liquid rubber or unique molds found right in your own home; or by browsing through any dime or hardware store. A little imagination is required to visualize how these items may be used to create a novelty candle, but that's all part of the creative challenge of candle making.

Let's look at a few of these improvised molds and see just how each one may be used to create a conversation piece.

DIXIE CUPS

These and other similar paper containers may also be used to form small novelty type candles for table settings, mantel arrangements, and such. The wick may be secured the same way as was done with the paper cones or, because of the flat base, a wick tab may be used to weight the wick down rather than extending it through a hole at the base.

PAPER CONES

These are used to form small candles resembling hats, trees, mountains, faces, etc. (See Picture 4). Here's how:

Insert the wick. (See Figure 32).

Place the cone in a tall glass or can containing cold water so that the wax will "set up" immediately and retard dripping through the wick hole. (See Figure 33).

When the wax has hardened, the paper will probably have to be torn off unless the mold was oiled with a salad or cooking oil prior to casting. Even then, the mold may have to be torn away.

METAL KITCHEN MOLDS

Count the number of different-shaped kitchen molds available and you have an idea of the number of candles that can be created from this group. The list includes such items as jello molds, pie and cake tins, muffin tins, etc.

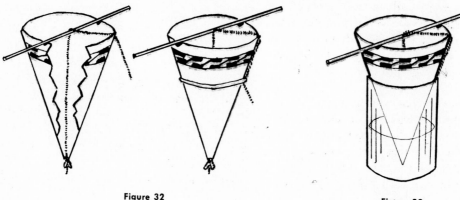

Figure 32   Figure 33

When using kitchen molds, it is wise to swab the interior of the mold with a vegetable oil before using, thus assuring easy release of the candle.

It is possible to actually create two different-shaped candles with one kitchen mold. Using a simple jello mold, Figures 34-A and 34-B illustrates the two candles that are formed from this single mold.

The way the candle sits will determine the method you will use to insert the wick. For instance, if your candle is to resemble Figure 34-A, the bottom of the candle corresponds with the bottom of the mold and, therefore, the wick does not have to be exposed. Consequently, the weighted wick method described heretofore would be used. After the wick has been inserted you proceed as follows:

Pour in the wax and place the mold in a warm water bath, being careful to keep the water from running over the top edge of the mold into the wax.

As the wax cools, a small well will form; this may or may not be filled, depending on its size. For smaller molds, filling the well is not necessary, but when using large molds, the well might require a "refill."

When the wax has hardened, remove the wick holder, withdraw the candle from the mold, and you have a unique novelty candle. Most small-floating candles are made this way.

If you wish your candle to resemble Figure 34-B, you obviously can't use a wick tab or weight to secure your wick, since it would show at the top of the finished candle and the wick wouldn't protrude out of the wax. Therefore, the wick must be secured by other means, such as the coiled wick method, or the drilled hole method.

GLASS MOLDS

Here again the opportunities for creating candles are unlimited. Some of the glass containers you probably have right in your own kitchen that can be used for candle molds include ordinary drinking glasses, cocktail, juice, pilsner, sherbet and shot glasses; votive glasses, bowls, coffee cups, and custard cups. (See Figure 35).

The procedure for using these glass containers is much the same as that prescribed for kitchen metal molds, except special care must be taken to prevent glass breakage by hot wax. Two added precautions will alleviate this problem: (1) Just prior to pouring the wax, run hot water over the exterior of the glass. (2) Pour the wax at a low temperature, approximately 160°.

Note that the glass containers are all shaped so that the open end is widest, permitting easy release of the hardened wax. Other glass containers (where the open end has the smallest span) can be used for candle molds, but these must be broken to remove the candle. All types of inexpensive bottles can be used to create unusual candles. Normally the neck of the bottle is not filled with wax, because the glass is generally thickest at this end, making it difficult to remove without destroying the "wax neck."

Picture 4

Figure 34-A

Figure 34-B

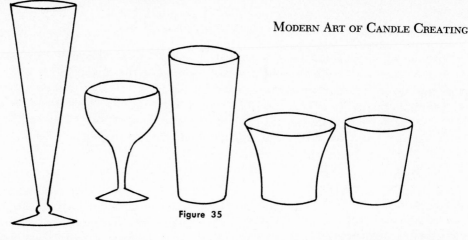

Figure 35

There are two popular methods with which to break the bottles safely so as to expose the finished candle.

Cold method—When the wax has completely hardened, wrap the bottle in a tea towel or cloth bag, immerse in cold water, and tap gently with a hammer. Open the towel and "peel" off the pieces of glass.

Hot method—If the glass is thin, freeze in the refrigerator about eight hours. Again, wrap the bottle in a tea towel or cloth bag and plunge it into boiling water. The thermal shock will fracture the glass and allow safe removal.

After the bottle has been removed from the candle, there might be some unsightly marks left on the candle surface. These can be diminished or eliminated entirely by either immersing the candle in a hot water bath or a hot wax bath.

By pouring two identical wax figures from the same mold and joining the two wax "halves," you produce a completely different shaped and frequently more attractive candle. (See Figure 36).

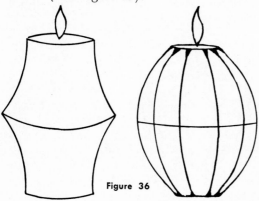

Figure 36

Frank Bowley, of Smethport, Pennsylvania, has his own method for joining two "halves" to make a ball-shaped candle. He uses a round jello mold to make the two sides of the ball. When the two halves are out of the mold he joins them in the following manner: "Heat the flat side of the two halves with an electric iron on edge and stick them together. Drill a hole down the center, insert the wick. Fill around the wick with hot wax to hold it in place, then dip a couple of times in hot wax (about 230°F)." Mr. Bowley states he has made hundreds of candles this way and they not only stick together, but finish up so the seam does not show.

PLASTIC MOLDS

With the advent of synthetics and plastics, many home items previously made of metal or glass are now made of these new materials. It is thus understandable why many candle hobbyists find themselves using plastic molds as well as metal and glass. The shapes are the same and so is the method of pouring the mold. One item should be mentioned, however. Some plastic containers, such as drinking glasses or cups, can stand extreme heat, while other plastic containers cannot absorb hot liquid. Therefore, pour the wax as cool as possible for the latter group.

Another method of making a ball-shaped candle, this time out of plastic, comes from Mary Pruden, of Riverdale, New Jersey:

"Stiff plastic balls from the dime store are available in many sizes. With a razor blade,

Picture 5

cut them in half along the seam line. Set them in a pan of sand or borax to keep them steady and level. Pour the wax right to the top rim, and refill the center as necessary. If the wax *humps* above the center, trim it level with a hot knife. When the wax has hardened, it will slip easily out of the *mold.*" Mrs. Pruden's description of how she inserts the wick in this type of candle was given earlier. After the wick has been inserted, pare down the bottom to give a good flat base.

Mrs. Pruden goes on to say: "If the halves are carefully joined and trimmed, a quick dip into hot wax will give them a finish so they can be turned into glamorous Christmas balls with glitter, sequins, pearls, stones and broken jewelry."

The development of plastics has contributed immensely to the production of numerous new products on the market. Such a product is the new two-piece plastic mold designed and manufactured specifically for creating novelty candles. Since detailed instructions accompany each of these molds, there is no need to duplicate the instructions here. However, some of the different shapes available are shown in Picture 5.

RUBBER MOLDS

With a relatively new product called Liquid Rubber now available, it is possible to create wax figures or candles from irregular shaped forms. Formerly, if a mold couldn't be opened to release the hardened wax, or, if the candle couldn't slide out one end, the form was considered impossible to use as a candle mold. But, thanks to liquid rubber, this is no longer true and any hobbyist may now create irregular wax forms or candles using virtually any small object he desires—solid or hollow. This is how it works: With a small brush, apply four or five coats of liquid rubber to the object you wish to duplicate in wax, letting each coat dry before applying the next. After the final coat has set completely, pull back the rubber coating, removing it completely from the original form, leaving a hollow, flexible rubber mold. With this mold you can now create exact replicas of your original form merely by pouring in wax and peeling off the rubber mold when the wax has hardened; simple when you have the right materials, but impossible if you don't. (See Picture 6.)

Picture 6

CONTAINER TYPE CANDLES

These candles, often called patio candles since they were used originally outdoors, are candles left right in their glass molds to be burned. Here again there is no limit on what can be used for a container. Those mentioned previously as glass molds, in addition to numerous others whose shapes are unique, may be used to produce exceptionally striking displays. "Glass brick" candles, for instance, are extremely eye-catching, while glasses with stems are particularly popular in that they raise the candle above an arrangement of greens. In many cases, the container itself is decorated with decals, glitter, paint, sequins and such to enhance its beauty. (See Picture 7.)

As this type of candle is contained in a glass, it is not only decorative but functional as well. Let's list some of its advantages.

Dripless. Unless wax learns how to run uphill there's no possible way for these candles to drip. The melted wax remains completely confined within the container, thereby permitting the candle to be placed directly on table tops with no danger of unsightly, destructive running wax. That's one of the reasons they're so popular at restaurants as table lights.

Countless containers. Anything goes with a container candle as far as the shape of the container is concerned. All glasses, regardless of shape or size, vases, mugs, cups— there's no end. The only restriction is that the opening of the container must permit proper draft conditions to allow the flame to burn without smoking.

Decorator's delight. Particularly those containers with smooth exteriors offer numerous decorating possibilities. Decals, stickers,

Picture 7

Courtesy of Better Homes and Gardens

Container type candles created in ordinary household receptacles

sequins, glitter, jewelry, paint—they're all easy to use and very effective on any glass container.

Lasting feature. Once the container is decorated, it stays that way until the wax is consumed inside. No redecorating is necessary; just repour wax into the container when needed.

Durability. Many container candles, particularly the wide, deep, round ones, are wonderful candles for outdoor use. These are called patio lamps. Because of their protected flame, they're much like hurricane lamps.

These candles are poured exactly the same way as the glass-molded candles described previously, the only difference being that the candle is left in the container.

To create an exceptionally attractive container-type candle or patio candle, simply stretch a length of plastic netting over any glass with a diameter of from two to four inches. This netting is available from Pourette and enables the candle hobbyist to create patio candles identical to those found in all candle shops. (See Picture 8.) Any plain drinking glass can be transformed into an eye-catching candle by merely painting the glass, pouring in the wax, inserting the wick and applying the netting.

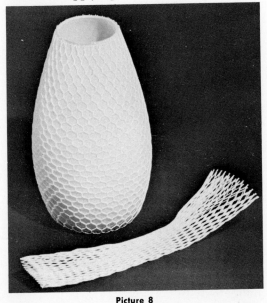

Picture 8

HURRICANE CANDLES

This particular type is relatively new in the candle field and bears little resemblance to the other three types, except they are created of wax. A *hurricane candle* is actually a "shell" of wax, either round or square, within which is placed a votive glass and votive candle. When the votive candle is lit, the light glows through the sides of the *hurricane candle*, producing a beautiful and cheerful display. (See Pictures 66 and 67.)

These candles are similar to container-type candles in many respects. There is no dripping problem; they provide numerous decorating possibilities and can be used indefinitely. Unlike the container-type candle, however, *hurricane candles* are somewhat limited in shape. Since the "shell" of wax must be withdrawn from a mold, their shapes are confined to only those molds which permit release of the "shell." In addition, the mold should be at least four inches across to permit the votive light in the center to burn without melting the sides.

Pourette has four molds designed specifically for *hurricane candles*. Many forms found in your home also qualify as molds for these unique candles. Large jello molds, two-quart milk cartons, cardboard paint buckets and mixing bowls are just a few of the large improvised molds that may be used. Follow these directions for making *hurricane candles*:

Melt and color your wax in the usual manner.

When the wax temperature reaches 190° pour it slowly into the mold until filled to within ½″ of the top. (See Figure 37.)

Figure 37

Place the mold carefully in a water bath and weight down with a heavy object to prevent the mold from floating and tipping.

Allow the mold to set in the bath until a film about ⅛″ has formed over the surface of the wax (the walls of the candle should be about ¼″ thick at this time).

Remove the mold from the bath; insert a paring knife through the surface film parallel with and about ¼″ from the edge of the mold; cut out and remove the center film. (See Figure 38.)

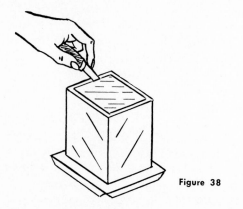

Figure 38

Pour out the excess melted wax, leaving a "shell" of congealed wax about ¼″ thick. (See Figure 39.)

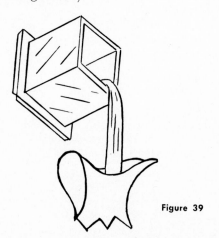

Figure 39

For the taller *hurricanes* it is advisable to secure a round cookie-cutter on the end of a stick or dowel and, while the bottom of the "hurricane shell" is still soft, press the cutter through the soft wax to the metal base. (See Figure 40.) When the shell is

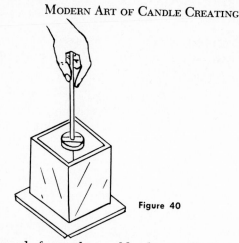

Figure 40

removed from the mold, the small "wax cookie" is snapped out of the bottom, allowing the *hurricane candle* to be placed over the votive candle, rather than having to lower the votive candle down the inside.

Allow the "wax shell" to cool until ready to withdraw from the mold. With the shell out of the mold, place a votive candle in a votive glass in the center of the *hurricane* shell; when lit, it will glow through the sides of the candle. (See Figure 41.)

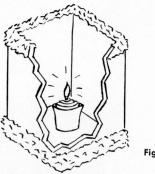

Figure 41

Only a high temperature wax of approximately 140° to 150° should be used in creating a *hurricane candle* to enable the "shell" to withstand the heat of the votive candle flame. Even then it is recommended that it be burned for only about two hours at a time to prevent any softening of the sides. While burning, it is advisable to place this type of candle away from drafts to avoid blowing the flame toward one side. Consequently, *hurricane candles* normally make poor patio candles due to their vulnerability to drafts.

Potential Troubles: Causes and Remedies

A candle hobbyist occasionally produces a defective candle; one, say, that refuses to burn properly. Perhaps the candle frustratingly will not even release from the mold.

Fortunately, for every problem there is a remedy.

That's what this chapter is all about—the reasons for candle defects.

Assuming you are using tried-and-tested waxes, colors, wicking and the like—and are still experiencing imperfections – then the following information may help.

BLOCK CANDLES USING ONE-PIECE MOLD

PROBLEM 1: CANDLE WON'T RELEASE FROM MOLD

Possible reasons:

Wax too soft. As soft wax cools it contracts away from the top-center, leaving a large depression around the wick. With harder waxes, the wax contracts more quickly and uniformly, allowing greater contraction away from the mold walls. Harder wax also has poor adhesion properties—an advantage, in this case.

Wax cooled too slowly. When slow cooling, wax is able to collapse in the vertical direction at a slower pace; hence, total horizontal contraction is decreased.

Wax overflowed the "well" during the refilling process. If liquid wax flows between the mold wall and the candle, the release will understandably be adversely effected.

The mold itself doesn't permit release. Any mold which has an undercut prohibiting release or a portion where the diameter exceeds the diameter at the opening of the mold prohibiting release, then such a mold, of course, should not be used.

PROBLEM 2: CANDLE MOTTLES

This is a desired feature for many candle makers; for others, it is not. Therefore, we feel the reasons for this effect should be considered here for the latter.

Possible reasons:

Wax is too hard. As the hard wax cools, the small air bubbles are immobilized, giving increased mottling.

Wax cooled too slowly. Slower cooling causes larger crystals to form and split up more easily. In addition, the slow cooling allows these large crystals to form near the walls of the mold, thereby making the mottling more noticeable.

Too much oil added. Oil is known to weaken bulk wax, encouraging rifts within the candle. The result is the mottled appearance. (See Picture 9.)

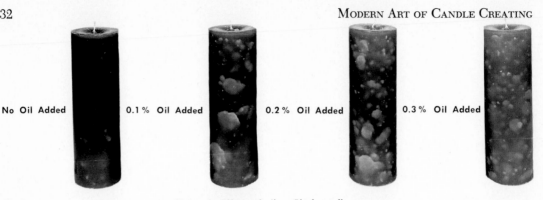

No Oil Added   0.1% Oil Added   0.2% Oil Added   0.3% Oil Added

Picture 9—Effects of oil on Block candles

PROBLEM 3: FRACTURES APPEAR WITHIN THE CANDLE

Possible reasons:

Wax was cooled too rapidly. The thermal-stresses acting on a wax are applied quicker, causing fractures. This defect normally occurs when the candle and mold are:

Immersed in cold water.

Placed in the refrigerator too soon or too long.

Placed in the deep freeze.

The "well" was refilled after the wax in the mold had hardened.

PROBLEM 4: "FROST" MARKS APPEAR ON CANDLE SURFACE

These scaly, chalky streaks seem to occur because of excessive adhesion between the wax and the mold walls. This happens most frequently with square candles (where the mold walls can bend inward easily); infrequently with round candles.

Possible reasons:

Wax was not hot enough when poured. If the temperature is below 180° at the time of pouring, these "frost" marks are likely to occur.

Mold was too cold at the time of casting. The mold should be at least room temperature.

PROBLEM 5: SHALLOW POCK MARKS OR DEPRESSIONS APPEAR ON CANDLE SURFACE

Possible reasons:

Wax was poured at a temperature exceeding 212°. This causes the minute mois-

ture particles clinging along the interior mold wall to vaporize and form pockets of expanding steam. As the wax cools and the steam condenses, the depressions in the wax formed by the steam remain to blemish the candle surface. This problem is most prevalent with a new mold which has been sprayed with Silicone. The Silicone coating causes the pockets of steam to expand inward toward the center of the candle, rather than outward, thus making the pockets deeper and more noticeable.

Surface pock marks caused by slow cooling, especially during hot weather. Under very slow cooling conditions, these pock marks degenerate into large, ill-shaped, flat depressions.

PROBLEM 6: SMALL "PIT MARKS" APPEAR ON CANDLE SURFACE

Possible reasons:

Wax was poured into the mold too fast. This causes a turbulence, forming small air bubbles throughout the wax. Should these small bubbles become trapped along the mold wall, they result in tiny holes or "pit marks."

Dust particles were inside mold at time of pouring.

PROBLEM 7: WAX CHIPS AWAY AT BASE OF CANDLE

Possible reasons:

The "well" was filled too high. This is particularly true when a hard wax is used or when either lustre crystals or stearic acid is added to the wax. When the wax is re-poured and the level is brought right up to the edge of the top ridge, this ridge will tend to chip away after the candle is withdrawn from the mold. This is due to the poor adhesion between the extending hard ridge of wax and the wax used in repouring the well.

Mold kept in refrigerator too long. The extreme thermal shock causes the wax to become brittle. Small chips breaking off at the edges is the result.

Too many lustre crystals added. As has been mentioned, this additive is very effective as a wax-hardener. Too much, however, causes brittleness, again resulting in the wax chipping.

PROBLEM 8: SMALL, BUBBLY LINES ENCIRCLE THE CANDLE

Reason:

These are water-level lines and occur either when the level of the "bath" water is not above the wax level or when the water is added after the mold is inserted in the "bath."

PROBLEM 9: CANDLE SMOKES EXCESSIVELY

This is always due to incomplete combustion caused by inadequate mixture of oxygen and wax.

Possible reasons:

Wick too large. This was discussed thoroughly in the section on wicking, but we'll review it briefly. If the wick is too large, the flame consumes the wax faster than the wick can absorb it. This lack of fire results in incomplete combustion, causing excessive smoking. This smoking can usually be eliminated by trimming the wick periodically.

Candle burning in draft. Any turbulence of air around a flame will hinder complete combustion.

Lack of fuel (wax). To burn properly, the wick must be surrounded by a small pool of liquid wax from which to absorb fuel for the flame. Should this pool become dry, the candle will smoke momentarily until the fuel is replenished. Three situations may leave this cup dry. They are:

When the candle is first lit and has not had an opportunity to provide enough liquid wax to feed the flame.

After the pool of wax broaches the edge and drips out, the cup is momentarily left with no "fuel."

If any cavities were left inside the candle, these voids may drain away the melted wax, again leaving the flame with little fuel with which to maintain complete combustion.

PROBLEM 10: CANDLE DRIPS EXCESSIVELY

Possible reasons:

Wax is too soft. This results in the wax melting too rapidly for the flame to consume. The excess wax consequently broaches the candle edge and drips.

Too many lustre crystals added. Though they harden wax, too much may induce a candle to drip.

Metal core wick was used. This wick is often used purposely in tapers to force dripping.

Wick too small. As previously mentioned in the section on wicking, if the wick is too small to absorb the wax melted by the flame, the sides of the candle will broach, causing an overflow, or drip.

PROBLEM 11: CANDLE "SPLATTERS" WHILE BURNING

Reason:

The voids or cavities which form in the center of the candle were not re-poured. As the wick burns down, the air in these cavities expands due to the heat from the flame. When the wax film separating the flame and the cavity is such that it can no longer contain the expanding air, the heated air bursts through the thin wax film, causing wax to splatter.

PROBLEM 12: CANDLE HAS A "DITCH" OR "CAVE-IN" ON THE SIDE

Reason:

The "well" was not poked soon enough. Since wax contracts as it cools, void areas are formed within the candle and actually set up a vacuum at the outset. If this vacuum remains during the setting-up period, the air pressure from outside the wax walls will force the wax in, resulting in a "ditch" in the finished candle. To prevent this, the vacuum seal must be broken by poking holes through the "well" and allowing the entrance of air to equalize the air-pressure from without.

CONTAINER-TYPE CANDLES

PROBLEM 1: EXCESSIVE SMOKING

Possible reasons:

Deep in these containers, the flame is too large for the available oxygen supply. The wick should be decreased.

Any of the other reasons given previously for this problem with the block candles should be explored.

PROBLEM 2: UNMELTED WAX IS LEFT STICKING TO THE INSIDE OF THE CONTAINER

Possible reasons:

The candle is burned intermittently. Such spasmodic burning does not allow all the wax within the "melting range" to melt as it ordinarily would under an extended burning period.

Wax had too high a melting point. With a higher temperature wax, the "melting area" is decreased, thus leaving the unmelted wax sticking to the inside of the container.

HURRICANE CANDLES

PROBLEM 1: EXCESSIVE SMOKING

Possible reasons are the same as those listed for container-type and block candles.

PROBLEM 2: SIDES OF "SHELL" SAG

Possible reasons:

Wax used to create "shell" had too low a melting point. Hence, it had little resistance to the heat from within.

Votive candle was not centered on the "hurricane" base. Consequently the side of the "shell" closest to the flame becomes extremely vulnerable to over-heating.

Candle placed in draft. Such a condition is liable to cause the flame to "lick" towards one side of the "shell," causing that side to become unduly soft.

Candle left burning too long. By checking the "hurricane shell" occasionally you can observe if any of the sides are becoming soft. If this is the case, it is best to put out the flame until the shell of wax regains its hardness.

PROBLEM 3: VOTIVE LIGHT MELTS THROUGH FLOOR OF SHELL

Possible reasons:

The votive candle was not placed in a votive glass. Always use a glass to contain the votive candle, or the wax is apt to continue melting right through the "hurricane" bottom.

Votive candle overheated the votive glass. This occurs when the votive candle burns all the way down and exposes the glass bottom to excessive heat. The heated glass will ultimately melt the floor of the *hurricane candle,* unless the votive candle is replaced before it burns to the glass bottom.

PROBLEMS RESULTING DURING STORING PERIOD

When a beautiful candle has been created you'll certainly want it to stay that way, at least until it is used, sold, or given away. Here are a few hints and suggestions that will prove helpful.

PROBLEM 1: SURFACE BLEMISHES APPEAR ON FINISHED CANDLES

Remedy:

This is due usually to excessive handling. To restore the sheen, buff lightly with an old silk stocking, felt or a wax cloth. Hard waxes respond particularly to this treatment, but with soft waxes, the polishing action might result in considerable "plowing" of the surface.

PROBLEM 2: CANDLE BECOMES SOILED

Remedy:

Mary Pruden of Riverdale, New Jersey, offers this suggestion: "Apply plain cold cream or baby oil on a soft rag; junior's threadbare flannel pajamas are hard to beat. If the candle is very soiled, apply the cream or oil with your fingers, let stand a few moments, then gently polish with the rag. I spray many of my candles with a clear spray. This prevents them from finger marking."

Once you have created a candle which must be stored for a period of time, put it in a plastic bag or wrap it in Saran wrap. Then you won't have to worry about it becoming soiled or blemished due to handling.

PROBLEM 3: PIMPLES AND BLISTERS APPEAR ON STORAGE

Remedy:

Next time store your finished candles in a cool place. If stored in a warm temperature the wax becomes too soft, causing the air in the candle to combine into small bubbles or "pimples" on the candle surface.

From this discussion it is obvious that you must adhere strictly to proper instructions, materials and equipment to reduce the chance of difficulty. We all learn from experience, of course, and occasionally a candle won't turn out the way you had hoped, regardless of how careful you were. By understanding the possible reasons for a problem, you will be much better equipped to correct the trouble next time.

PART III

CANDLE CREATING AND
DECORATING TECHNIQUES

Pouring, Shaping Techniques for Unique Effects

So far we have given you an explanation of how to make a variety of candles suitable for any special occasion. Still, a candle, by its very nature, is a beautiful sight and many hobbyists prefer to leave it in its original form—undecorated.

There are those, of course, who, with the extra knowledge of pouring and shaping techniques, want something fancier found in the multi-colored, novel-shaped candles. Even these creations are rarely decorated, however, because any embellishment might only detract from their fascinating, bizarre appearance.

Now, let's review some of the exquisite numbers that you, yourself, can make.

CHUNK CANDLES

Perhaps a more appealing name would be *marbleized* or *variegated* candles, but, since wax chunks are the main ingredients, we'll continue to call them *chunk candles* for easy recognition. A brief definition of this candle might be "a combination of colored wax chunks and liquid wax in a candle to obtain a varied colored effect." (See Group Picture IV, Page 80d.) There are several offshoots originally derived from the

ordinary *chunk candle* which we'll discuss one by one, but first let's see how a regular chunk candle is made.

SOURCE OF WAX CHUNKS

The first requirement for any *chunk candle* is to have a supply of wax chunks on hand. Many hobbyists save all the excess wax after each candle-pouring so that, when chunks are needed, colored wax is already available to break up. Perhaps you have some old candles around that are ready for remelting. Break them up. Even old tapers may be used if they are colored clear through and the wicks are removed.

If you don't have the desired colored wax on hand with which to make your chunks, then, of course, you will have to make some. Here's how it's done: When the melted wax has been colored and ready for pouring, follow either of these two courses:

Broken Chunk Method. Pour the colored wax into any mold, let it harden and withdraw. Place this colored wax block in a large cardboard box placed on a sturdy table. Proceed to break this wax bulk into irregular small chunks (approximately 1½″ across) with a large hunting knife or chisel and a hammer, using the same technique as a diamond cutter. (See Figure 42.) In other words, place the cutting instrument (knife or chisel) on the wax where you wish to cut it, and then hit it sharply and firmly with the hammer.

Figure 42

Ice Cube Tray Method. Pour the colored wax into an ice cube tray (the plastic ones seem to work best because they release the wax easier than the metal ones). After the wax has cooled, remove the wax cubes from the tray.

Choose any metal mold you wish (since the wax must be poured quite hot—approximately 240°—a metal mold withstands the heat best) and insert the wick as described previously.

Now that your chunks are ready and your mold has the wick in it (no liquid wax yet), the next step is to drop the chunks into the mold. (See Figure 43.) While "packing" the

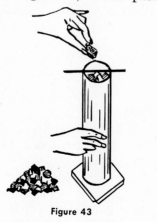

Figure 43

mold, don't attempt to fill all the voids or pack the chunks too tightly. In fact, the more open spaces, the easier it is for the liquid wax to reach and fill all the void areas, thereby making a smoother, more solid burning candle.

Several methods can be employed in arranging the wax chunks, depending on the desired effect of the finished candle. They may be dropped in systematically, according to a set color scheme, or in a "helter-skelter" fashion; chunks solely of one color or several colors may be used; other materials, such as leaves and greens, may be added to show through the outside surface of the finished candle.

Regardless of the plan you use in positioning the chunks, which we'll discuss at greater length later, the final steps in creating your *chunk candle* are similar to any other candle. Uncolored melted wax at a temperature of at least 230° is poured slowly into the mold until it is filled. As the wax is poured you'll note a slight settling of the chunks in the mold, making it necessary to drop in a few extra near the end of the pouring to fill the mold's upper span. To meet this "emergency," it is best to have a few extra chunks nearby for a quick "refill."

Chunk candles should be water-cooled in a warm bath, the same as any other candle cast in a metal mold. A small well will form. This should be "poked" to relieve the surface tension, but with chunk candles it is necessary to fill the well only once with melted wax, not two or three times as in the case of regular molded candles.

There are several methods employed in "packing" chunks to achieve various effects. Following are the most popular techniques.

TECHNIQUES USED IN APPLYING CHUNKS

Multi-Colored Chunk Candle. This method uses chunks of at least two or more colors, chosen to match the season, occasion or surroundings. How these chunks are arranged determines the type of multi-colored candle. Three main "plans" of chunk-arranging for a multi-colored *chunk candle* follow:

Interspersed plan. Drop the chunks into the mold, following no definite pattern or arrangement to achieve a marbleized effect.

Horizontal layers. If you want all the chunks of one color to remain together in definite layers, determine the desired width of the layers and drop in the chunks accordingly. For instance, if your mold is twelve inches tall, drop in four inches of red chunks, four inches of white and four inches of blue and your finished candle will be three definite layers of red, white and blue—a very beautiful Fourth of July display.

Vertical layers. Once more your chunks are definitely arranged in colored groupings, but in vertical layers, not horizontal. This necessitates making a temporary partition between the various colors to prevent them from intermingling. Figure 44 illustrates a simple but effective partition made of cardboard for a four-colored vertical-layered *chunk candle*. Once this partition is placed in the mold each of the four colors is dropped in its own section. (See Figure 45.) After the mold has been "packed" with the chunks, the partition is removed, leaving the chunks joined in vertical layers.

Figure 44

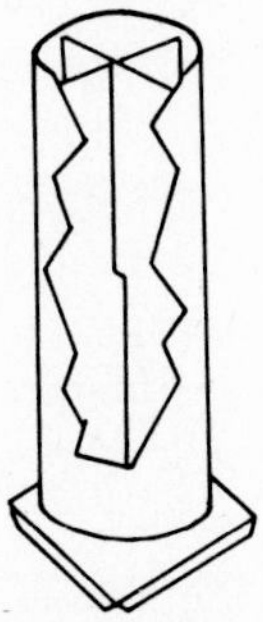

Figure 45

Single-Colored Chunk Candle. Using chunks all of one color is the easiest of the *chunk candles* to create, yet the effect is still wonderfully unique. A two-colored appearance may be attained simply by coloring the melted wax any pastel shade other than the color of the chunks.

Chunk Candle with Interior Decorations. This is one of the most interesting candles there is, at the same time surprisingly simple to make. Choose something from "Mother Nature's Variety Store," such as leaves, ferns or flowers—something relatively flat-surfaced. Using small (approximately ¾″) uncolored white chunks, begin packing your mold until it is about a third full. Then insert your "decoration" along the inside mold wall and continue "packing." As your chunks rise they will act as a support, keeping the decoration pressed firmly against the mold wall. When you are satisfied that the decoration is well situated in relation to location and closeness to the mold wall, proceed to fill the void areas with clear melted wax. Let the mold set for about a minute to permit any air bubbles to escape to the surface before placing it in your warm water bath. (See Picture 10.)

That's all there is to it.

Picture 10

White Chunks with Bits of Coloring. Try this one for an extraordinary display. While packing white wax chunks into your mold, drop in small bits of wax coloring next to the mold wall at varying levels. Experiment with this technique, using various color combinations, or try different color placements. Each candle will be different. (See Group Pictures I and II, Pages 80a and 80b.)

DECORATING CHUNK CANDLES

Though these candles are decorative as are, if a decoration is desired use a very simple one, such as these two suggested by Hazel Clampitt of St. Paul, Minnesota:

With glitter cement make two or three dots about ¼" across and put a small stone (from junk jewelry) or a colored glass bead in the center of each dot. On the cement around the stone or bead, sprinkle diamond dust.

Make four to six large dots with glitter cement and sprinkle with diamond dust; tends to sparkle like rhinestones.

COLORED-LAYER CANDLES

This technique merely involves pouring liquid wax of varying colors at different time intervals. The results are quite novel. Perhaps you have seen a rainbow candle containing all the colors of the rainbow—yellow, orange, red, burgundy, orchid, blue, light and dark green. This was created via the following age-old technique:

String the wick as previously described.

Melt enough wax and color it the shade you want at the *top* of your candle. (Remember, the wax at the bottom of the mold normally becomes the top of your candle.)

Determine the width of your color band and pour in the first color. A simple way to measure the width accurately is by putting your ruler to good use.

Extend the ruler into the mold until it reaches the bottom; hold it against the side of the mold. (See Figure 46.)

Mark the ruler at the point of insertion. If you wish the colored band to have a

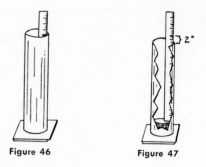

Figure 46   Figure 47

2" width, slide the ruler 2" up the side of the mold and hold.

Pour in your wax (at about 180°) until the wax level reaches the bottom of the ruler—and you have the 2" band. (See Figure 47.)

Let this first wax layer harden completely before pouring in the second color. With each separate pouring repeat the process until the desired height of your candle is attained.

Often these candles emerge with small ridges encircling the candle at the point where the colors join. These ridges are not unsightly and do little to impair the beauty of the candle, but if you must eliminate them, a quick dip in very hot wax (230°) will smooth over the surface. With a wax dip, your colored bands will not be as intense, but this too is often desired.

There is absolutely no limit to the color schemes possible in pouring one of these colored-layer candles. You also have at least three choices as to the position of your colored bands. They are:

HORIZONTAL LAYERS

(See Figure 48.) Simply leave the mold standing vertically and pour in the desired colors to form horizontal colored bands.

ANGLED LAYERS

(See Figure 49.) Position your mold at an angle while pouring. This means a wider warm water bath container, such as a tub, is necessary to provide enough room for the mold to be tilted. Hold your mold at a constant angle by positioning two blocks of wood, or similar supports, at locations which

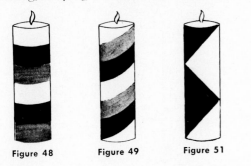

Figure 48   Figure 49   Figure 51

provide support for your mold as illustrated in Figure 50.

ALTERNATING ANGLED LAYERS

(See Figure 51.) Position your mold at an angle while pouring, but reverse the angle of the mold for each pouring.

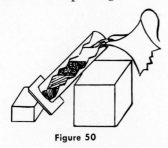

Figure 50

COLOR BLENDED CANDLES

These candles are similar to the colored-layer candles but with one exception. The various colors are poured into a wax "shell" within the mold. This might sound complicated, but it is actually quite simple and enables you to create a multi-colored candle in which the colors are very subtly blended together. Here's how:

String your wick as described in the section on wicking.

Fill the mold with melted wax and allow it to set in a water bath for about ten to fifteen minutes, or until a thin coat of hardening wax appears around the inside walls of the mold.

Remove the mold from the water bath and pour out the remaining wax.

Let this "shell" of wax cool for about fifteen minutes.

Refill the inside with one or more colors.

When refilling the interior, pour the wax directly into the center of the mold, not down the side as normally. The reason is obvious. The hot wax "washing" against the side would melt the existing wax "shell" and ruin the appearance of the candle. A beautiful two-tone candle can be created by refilling the candle with a different colored wax from that used at the outset. The thickness of the shell is thinner at the top of the mold than at the bottom, enabling the color from the second pouring to partially melt and blend with this portion of the shell. A subtle two-tone effect is the result. (See Group Picture III, Page 80c.)

If uncolored wax is used to form the wax shell, pour several layers of various colors into the shell, using the same techniques employed with the colored-layer candles. The only difference will be in the intensity of the colored bands, for all colors within the shell will appear more subdued at the candle surface.

FILIGREE CANDLES

Such candles are very rarely seen, even in the most exclusive candle shops. As with multi-colored blended candles, this type requires the formation of a wax shell at the outset, though the wick is not inserted until later. But we are getting ahead of ourselves, so let's take it from the beginning.

Plug the wick hole at the base to prevent wax leakage or water seepage. Here's one way to accomplish this:

Thread about ¼" of wick through the wick hole and insert the wick retainer screw. The piece of wick will act as a gasket and hold the screw in place.

Tighten the screw until it is firmly secured in the hole and cut away any remaining wick.

Apply a large wad of mold sealer over the screw to assure a leakproof seal.

Fill the mold with liquid wax and place it in a warm water bath for approximately ten to fifteen minutes, or until a coating of wax about ¼" has formed around the inside walls of the mold.

Remove the mold from the water bath

and pour out the remaining liquid wax the same way you do when making a *hurricane candle.*

Set the mold aside until it is completely cold; remove the mold sealer, the screw, and the piece of wick, and remove the wax shell from the mold.

Drill a number of holes (approximately ½″ diameter) at various locations on the shell, and one in the center at the base through which the wick is inserted. If you do not have a drill, start these holes with an ice pick and widen them with a screw driver. (See Figure 52).

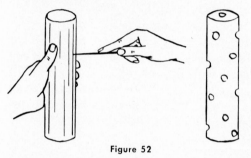

Figure 52

When the desired number of holes have been made, place the wax shell back into the mold, being very careful to line up the seam mark on the shell with the seam in the mold. This assures you that the wax is in the exact same position as it was prior to being removed.

String the wick as you normally would and refill the shell with melted wax of another color.

Refill the mold with wax of one color or pour layers of different colored wax, as was explained in the section on colored-layer candles.

When all the wax has hardened, remove the candle and view a most unique candle. The colors from within will show vividly through each hole, providing an intriguing, polka-dot effect. (See Figure 53.) (Also see Group Picture I, Page 80a.)

For a more dense, opaque wax shell, one that will subdue the colored interior more readily, add either stearic acid or Pourette luster crystals to the wax during the original pouring. Three tablespoons of stearic acid

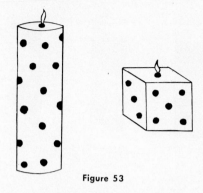

Figure 53

or half a tablespoon of luster crystals, mixed with one pound of wax, is adequate.

If you become proficient at carving, you needn't restrict yourself to making wax shell holes. Try various shapes, such as diamonds, flowers, trees, bells, etc. (See Figure 54).

Figure 54

CORRUGATED CANDLES

If you have some corrugated cardboard handy and feel like creating a very novel candle, try one of these.

Choose any large round or square cardboard mold and cut a piece of corrugated cardboard to fit inside so that the sides meet in a perfectly straight line when butted together.

Remove the cardboard and grease it thoroughly with unsalted fat (shortening).

Tape the sides of the cardboard together on the smooth side with masking tape, forming a hollow cylinder with the corrugations on the inside.

Reposition this corrugated cylinder into the "master" mold and insert the wick as usual. (See Figure 55).

Pour a thin layer (⅜″) of wax directly into the cylinder and let harden. This layer seals off the bottom of the cylinder and prevents wax from seeping outside the cylinder when the mold is poured.

Before the actual pouring, it is best to confine the mold to a bucket—just in case of trouble. A leaking or bursting cardboard mold can create quite a mess if not controlled. When all precautions have been taken, fill the interior of the corrugated cardboard with wax at a temperature of approximately 160°.

When the wax has completely hardened, strip the cardboard mold away from the corrugated cardboard. With a very sharp knife or razor blade make a slit down the side of the cardboard and peel it off, exposing the corrugated candle. (See Figure 56).

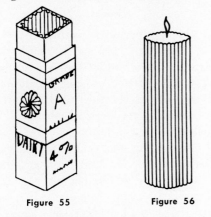

Figure 55   Figure 56

These corrugated candles will not have the sheen or gloss inherent in metal-molded candles, but their novel features compensate for this. A quick dip in a hot (230°) wax bath will result in a glossier finish, however.

ALUMINUM FOIL CANDLES

We've discussed thoroughly how colored wax chunks are placed in a mold to produce an unusual marbleized effect. Aluminum foil candles are made the same way, except crumpled aluminum foil is used instead of wax chunks. (See Group Picture I, Page 80a.)

Your first question, no doubt, is: "Would these candles actually burn with *balls* of aluminum foil lodged in the wax?" Yes, they

do, but as the candle burns down and exposes the foil, it must be picked out or trimmed so as not to obstruct the proper burning of the wick.

After stringing your mold with the proper wick, proceed as follows:

Cut out squares (approximately 6″ square) of aluminum foil and crumple them up *loosely* into wads about 3″ long and 1″ wide. Crumple them in such a way as to keep the shiniest side exposed as much as possible. (See Figure 57).

Figure 57

Push these aluminum "wads" into the mold, leaving the area surrounding the wick void of foil as much as possible. Be sure you don't press them in too tightly for you must leave adequate space in between the foil for the wax to seep.

Pour wax of any color into the mold (230°) and tap side of mold with a pencil to release any trapped air bubbles.

Place mold in water bath and proceed with cooling.

The Pourette Mfg. Co. and Lumi Lite Candle Co. have metalic foil available in numerous colors, making it possible to create even more spectacular displays.

HAND-CARVED CANDLES

By hand-carved candles we aren't referring to the type of carving that children do with soap. Though this could be done and no doubt very beautiful candles could be created in this manner, the tremendous amount of time and skill involved would make them too costly. So many molds are now available to create novel figures that there is little need for wax carvings.

What do we mean, then, by hand-carved candles? Two ideas come to mind: (1) The outlining of designs, patterns, letters and the like with a V-groover, and (2) the cutting out of a section along the lower side of the candle to form a "shadow box."

OUTLINE CARVING

The decorative possibilities are limitless if you have a little imagination and a knack for drawing.

For an intricate design it is wise to draw it first on a piece of tracing paper rather than directly on the candle. This eliminates the possibility of making a mistake on your candle and possibly ruining it. (See Figure 58).

When you are satisfied with the design on your tracing paper, simply position it over your candle and trace over the design with a ball-point pen. (See Figure 59).

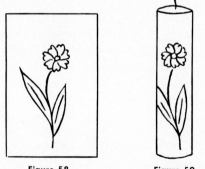

Figure 58	Figure 59

Remove the tracing paper, exposing the marks made with the pen, and you are ready to carve.

A regular V-groover, such as a linoleum carver, wood carver, or a V-shaped chisel, is necessary to do the carving properly. (See Figure 60).

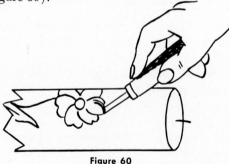

Figure 60

So as to make the design's grooves "stand out," they are usually colored before or after carving.

Pre-coloring method. Melt a small amount of wax and color it whatever color you prefer the outside of your candle to be. "Paint" this wax over the entire surface until the candle's original color is completely hidden. Allow this outer coating to harden and "set up" before carving. (See Figure 61).

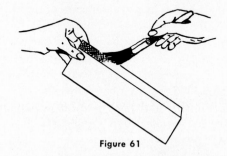

Figure 61

The thinner the outer coating, the easier it will be to carve and the better the final appearance. Therefore, it is advantageous to use very concentrated coloring for the outer coat; this eliminates the need of several coats to achieve the desired color.

Brushing the wax on the candle is preferred to dipping the candle in a colored wax bath, because the brushed wax adheres more readily and is less likely to break off while carving.

With the colored coating completely set, outline your candle design and commence carving. As the grooves outlining the design are gouged out, the color of the interior wax becomes exposed, thus giving a two- colored effect and producing a very fascinating and attractive candle. (See Figure 62 and Picture 67.)

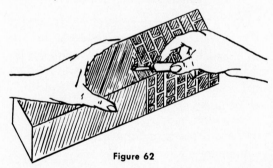

Figure 62

Subsequent-coloring method. This method provides the opportunity for a more varied and colorful design, since numerous colors can be employed. Simply carve the design and paint the grooves with a small brush, using a brush and paint that adheres to wax.

Another method that might be applied to create an artistic appearance is to spray the candle first with a gold or silver paint, gouge out a design and either leave it as is or paint the grooves another color.

Here is a "far out" hand-tooled candle that will catch the eye of all, yet it is exceptionally easy to create. You simply make a round or square block candle of any dark color (brown or black preferably), and while someone holds the candle firmly on a table, drag a hand saw, held cross-wise and at a 30° angle to the candle, down the length of the candle until all sides are "grooved." (See Figure 63). Then make similar grooves with the saw at a 45° angle to the initial grooves; the result looks uniquely like a surface of hand-tooled leather. (See Figure 64). Incidentally, if you should happen to create a candle with a blemished surface, this would be a good way to conceal the blemishes and yet create an attractive display. (See Picture 11).

SHADOW BOX CARVING

If you have a small figure or scene you wish to use for decorative purposes, this is an excellent way to incorporate it with your candle.

Make two cuts in your candle near the base with either a hacksaw or coping saw,

Picture 11   Picture 12

as shown in Figure 65, and withdraw the wax "plug."

Curve the upper slice with a knife to provide more room for your figure and improve the general appearance of the shadow box. (See Figure 66).

Smooth any rough edges off with a heated knife or spoon.

The surface of the wax inside the shadow box and around the edges may be decorated by applying paint glitter, whipped wax, etc.

Secure the decorative figure into the "box" with an adhesive of some sort, such as glue, glitter cement, lacquer or wax weld. (See Picture 12).

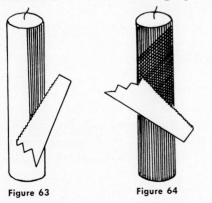

Figure 63   Figure 64

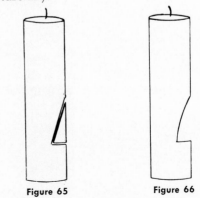

Figure 65   Figure 66

LIFE-LONG CANDLES

Too frequently the unfortunate part about candle creating is that the object of our creations must ultimately be consumed. Often a beautifully decorated candle has involved so much time, effort or expense that to burn it almost seems a sacrilege. You don't have to burn the candle, yet a candle isn't really "complete" nor does it attain its full beauty unless it is lit and given the opportunity to burn warmly and cheerfully.

What, then, is the answer? Usually there isn't any alternative but to burn it until consumed, thus, condemning it to the past. But in some cases it is possible and very practical to create a candle that can be burned indefinitely, with neither sacrifice of beauty nor consumption of wax. It's done with the aid of a votive glass or any small glass, jar or bottle.

This technique is best accomplished with a candle three inches or larger in diameter. If you are using a professional metal mold, such as a Pourette mold, you must first plug up the wick hole with tape or mold sealer. Do not insert wick; instead, place a small votive glass inverted in the bottom center of the mold before pouring the wax. (See Figure 67). Then pour the wax directly into the mold over the inverted glass and proceed with the usual method of cooling the wax. After removing the candle from the mold, you have a glass container imbedded in the top of the candle in which a votive candle can be burned. (See Figure 68). You may either buy votive candles ready-made to fit the glass, mold your own directly from the

glass beforehand, or refill the wax and replenish the wick as it burns down. The latter technique is not advised, however, because the hot wax being poured into the glass will likely cause the main candle wax to crack.

When your votive candle has been consumed you merely replace it with a new one without disturbing the main decorative candle. A simple technique, but highly practical. (See Group Picture I, Page 80a.)

Another and somewhat easier method of inserting a votive glass into the top of the candle is to burn a place for it. This is easily accomplished, particularly if you are using a hard wax. Merely make your candle in the normal manner and let it burn down to within about two inches from the top or the height of your glass container. Prevent the sides from melting by blowing out the candle at each burning before the sides become soft. With each lighting it will burn further down inside the candle, leaving the sides standing to conceal the container. When an adequate-sized hole has been acquired, insert the glass and votive candle—and your life-long candle is ready to burn.

One point of caution is necessary if you are doing this with a candle under 4″ in diameter. Burn the votive candle in the glass only about two hours at a time to prevent the votive glass from over-heating and melting the "concealing wall" of wax surrounding it.

This votive glass technique is very effective and much simpler to undertake if you make a candle with a diameter equal to that of a *hurricane candle* (6″ diameter). For one thing, the wide diameter makes it easy to locate the votive glass, whether you use the inverted technique or the melting-down method. There is also no danger of an over-heated votive glass melting down the concealing wall of wax due to its thickness. Finally, a candle with such a large diameter adapts naturally to this idea simply because it can't possibly melt and absorb the wax across its entire diameter. It can't help but "burn out" a hole in which you may insert the glass.

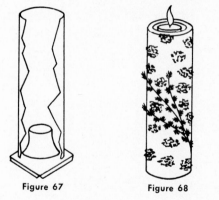

Figure 67   Figure 68

NOVEL CONTAINER-TYPE CANDLES

Container-type candles have the distinct advantage of giving the creator an opportunity to decorate and know that the decoration will not be consumed or damaged as the candle burns down. Therefore, quite artistic and clever creations are adaptable to this type of candle. Designs may be painted on, sequins may be glued on, glitter may be cemented on, and ornaments may be tied on.

You can even apply some of these decorations to the inside of the glass before the wax is poured. For instance, next time you pour a container candle try spraying the inside with glitter spray cement and add a generous sprinkling of glitter. You'll see this type of candle frequently around Christmas in your local department store, but you can certainly make your own at a far lesser cost.

You may even create a uniquely novel candle in a glass without any decoration. Sometime try this one: Fill a Pilsner glass ¾ full with a yellow-rust wax, insert wick and let set. Fill the remaining ¼ with whipped wax, spilling a little of the wax over one side. This candle looks so much like a foamy glass of beer that on a hot summer day you'll be looking at it longingly. (See Group Picture III, Page 80c.)

For a simple yet attractive gift, purchase two small tempo glasses. Make a candle out of one, leave one empty, but decorate both glasses the same way. The empty glass can be used as a cigarette holder and the candle becomes a matching cigarette lighter. This combination is a sure conversation piece on any coffee table. (See Picture 14).

Picture 14

Another novel idea utilizing a container-type candle was discovered in a small floral shop. The creator had inserted a votive glass in a brandy snifter filled with colorful "fried" marbles (available at most hobby shops). The flickering flame of the votive candle reflected the marbles, transmitting a sparkling array of colors. (See Picture 14-A).

Picture 14-A

INTERIOR-DECORATED CANDLE

Here is a candle-pouring technique that is in a class by itself for versatility and adaptability. Thus far, the pouring techniques described provide the means for creating unique candles but do not necessarily provide a new way for decorating candles. While these other techniques are certainly well worth knowing and serve a useful purpose, they limit themselves to a definite shape or appearance. The technique we are about to describe, however, opens up a whole new concept in candle-decorating; the possibilities for interesting, eye-catching creations are unlimited. No matter what the season or occasion, this method will enable you to create suitable candles.

By "Interior Decorated Candle" we mean precisely that—a candle decorated on the inside. This means that a large block candle mold or hurricane mold are a requirement, for you need ample area inside the mold to apply your decorations.

Follow the customary procedure in pouring your mold, whether it be for a hurricane candle or wick candle. Approximately ten minutes after you have poured the mold, remove it from your water bath, and pour the molten wax in the center back into your melting pot. The inside of your mold now has a thin layer (approximately ⅛") of wax and it is upon this wax coating that your decorations will be applied. If you aren't using a water bath during the setting-up period, allow a longer time to elapse before pouring out the molten wax to assure the formation of an adequate wax coating.

The question now arises, "What do we mean by decorations?" Two general items have been found to be particularly adaptable for decorative purposes—paper cut-outs, and bits of color buds. Since each of these is applied somewhat differently, for clarification we'll discuss the application of each one individually.

APPLICATION OF BITS OF COLORING

When applying bits of coloring you have the added option of creating either a speckled candle or a striped one. We'll undertake the speckled one first.

Immediately after the molten wax has been poured out, leaving a wax coating on the inside mold wall, sprinkle tiny bits of coloring over the inside area and press firmly into the soft wax. If a tall, block candle mold is used, it will be necessary to devise a means of scattering the colors evenly in the lower portion of the mold. One method is to place the colors on a ruler, hold the mold in a horizontal position, insert the "loaded" ruler into the mold, and shake off the coloring.

When the coloring application has been completed, refill the mold with wax at a temperature of 150°. At this low temperature, the colors will not melt and the result is a colorful speckled candle. (See Group Picture III, Page 80c.)

Should a bright-colored striped candle be more to your liking, it is necessary to apply the coloring in a different manner. Rather than sprinkling the coloring in a "hit-and-miss" fashion, you must press the desired colors by hand in a single line around the inside circumference of the mold, about ½" below the top edge of the wax. Refill the mold with wax at a temperature of 180°, a temperature high enough to partially melt the coloring before it sets up. As the coloring melts, it flows gently down the mold wall, leaving a colorful trail in its wake. The result is a colorful, striped candle. (See Group Picture III, Page 80c.)

Regardless of whether you desire a speckled candle or a striped one, you will want the colors to remain vivid and separate. Consequently, it is most important to know the exact temperature of the wax when repoured, for if it is too hot, the colors will melt completely, giving the candle a dark, muddy brown color.

After the mold has been "refilled," continue the normal cooling procedure until the candle is ready for withdrawal. If, however, you are forming a *hurricane candle*, pour the wax out again in approximately ten minutes to once more form your hurricane "shell."

APPLICATION OF PAPER CUT-OUTS

As with the color bits, your cut-outs should be ready for application immediately after the molten wax has been poured out. You must also work fast in order to complete your work while the wax coating is still soft. Whatever item you use in your interior decorating, it is imperative that it be pressed firmly *against* (but not *into*) the soft wax surface. This not only holds the decoration in place but assures uniform and clear viewing of the decoration through the wax coating.

Old Christmas cards, birthday cards, napkins, and magazine illustrations will provide you with unlimited decorating opportunities. When positioning your paper cut-outs in the mold, remember to insert them upside down because the top of your candle is normally at the bottom of your mold. (See Group Picture III, Page 80c.)

Once your "decoration" is firmly pressed against the wax "shell" you are ready for the final step. Simply repour the wax back into the mold at a temperature of 150° and let cool until ready to withdraw. Of course, if you are creating a *hurricane candle* you will have to pour this wax out again after approximately ten minutes to attain your hurricane wax shell.

HOW USED FOR THE VARIOUS HOLIDAYS

Here are a few suggestions as to how the Interior Decorated Technique can be utilized to create candles for special holidays.

Christmas. Red and green bits of coloring. Cut-outs from Christmas cards, such as nativity scenes, angels, Christmas trees, and ornaments.

New Year's. Apply a cut-out of a picture of the New Year Baby.

Valentine's Day. Apply red hearts cut from paper in a white candle.

St. Patrick's Day. Apply green shamrocks cut from paper in a white candle.

Fourth of July. Red and blue bits of coloring applied in a white candle to form stripes.

Halloween. Apply a black cat or witch cut from paper in an orange candle.

Thanksgiving. Apply a turkey cut from paper in rust or yellow candle.

Decorating Techniques Using Wax

Plain, undecorated candles are beautiful just as they are and often are left that way, with no decorations added to detract from their natural beauty. Some adornment, however, does enhance the beauty of most candles, if applied in good taste. Since candles are made of wax, it seems appropriate to many candle-makers that the decorations applied should also consist mainly of wax.

MOLTEN WAX DIP CANDLES

The term "molten wax dip" is self explanatory and requires little explanation. It is the process of dipping a candle into a liquid wax bath for the purpose of glazing or recoloring the surface. (See Picture 15).

A dipping vat is necessary, the size of which is dependent on the candle you wish to dip. It should be deep enough to permit complete submersion of the candle, and wide enough to allow at least one inch of liquid wax to surround the candle. An ideal dipping vat is made of a length of galvanized pipe or downspout soldered to a metal base. Most sheet metal shops carry a supply of pipe or downspout, ranging in diameter from 2″ to 10″, and will be happy to make a vat for you of any desired length.

There are a few things to remember when using a dipping vat. One, your candle displaces an equal amount of wax, causing the wax to rise considerably, particularly with a small diameter vat. Therefore, take this displacement law into consideration when preparing your wax bath. A good way to accurately determine the amount of liquid wax actually needed to envelop the candle is to first make a "test run" with water. Place the candle into the empty vat and pour in water until the candle is completely submerged. Mark the water level line and use this mark as a gage when filling the vat with wax. Incidentally, never dip the candle in wax until it is completely dry of water from the water test.

Picture 15—Two attractively glazed candles created by Mrs. Leona Harnden

The easiest way to insert the candle into the wax bath is by gripping the wick with pliers and not your fingers. This avoids the possibility of burning your fingers, particularly if the wick is quite short. Wait approximately a minute between each dip to allow time for each coating to "set up."

After the dipping operation has been completed, pour the remaining wax from the vat back into the melting pot for reuse. If left to harden in the vat, you will have quite a problem removing it.

As was mentioned previously, there are two basic reasons for dipping a candle. Here they are:

GLAZING PURPOSES

Perhaps you have created a candle with a few surface blemishes or have a whipped wax candle that you want smoothed over and given a glossy finish. This requires a dip in wax of at least 240° and normally requires only one or two dips. (See Picture 16.)

RECOLORING PURPOSES

If you want to recolor a candle or bring life back to a faded one, just "repaint" it with the aid of a dipping vat. For this purpose your wax should be approximately 190°, somewhat cooler than the wax prepared for glazing purposes. If the wax is too hot the coloring process takes longer to achieve; if too cool, the wax adhesion will be poor, causing blisters and bubbles on the candle surface.

A variety of color schemes can be acquired with the following technique: a single coating of a color differing from the candle-color itself; a multiple coating of varying colors dipped at different depths to reveal each color; a gradual shading from dark to light of one color by lowering the wax level on the candle with each successive dip.

Mrs. Harry Stalker of Bradenton, Florida, used this dipping method in creating candles for a District Flower Show. She writes: "I dipped most of my candles in one or more colors, first in a darker color, such as green, then yellow, etc., to obtain a color depth and give my candles personality. I also shaded some from dark at the bottom to light at the top."

WHIPPED WAX APPLICATION

Whipped wax applied to a candle surface is one of the most popular methods of decorating candles. Its snowy effect makes it particularly suitable for the Christmas season, but its light billowy appearance makes it equally popular during other seasons of the year. In fact, its uses are limitless. It may be applied over the whole candle (as shown in Picture 17); or on the larger portion of

Picture 16

Picture 17

the surface, leaving "windows" showing through (as in Figure 71); or in small "clusters" resembling clouds or ornaments (as illustrated in Figure 72). It may be applied uncolored (white) or colored to harmonize with the pattern of the candle. Ornaments, fruits, cones, leaves, and so forth can be inserted into it or it may remain as is. Different colored glitter may be sprinkled on for added effect, including diamond dust. This gives it "life" and the appearance of shimmering, glistening snow.

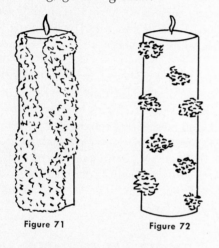

Figure 71   Figure 72

Incidentally, if you wish to color the whipped wax, the color should be added to the wax *before* it is whipped, though it may be tinted with a brush after the candle has been frosted. Remember, colored wax, when whipped, becomes much lighter due to the advent of air in the wax.

There's no doubt as to the uses and advantages of using whipped wax, but how is it formed and applied? The following basic steps constitute about all you must know when using whipped wax for decorative purposes on the candle itself.

Select a large can, such as a two-pound coffee can or gallon can, in which to melt your wax for whipping. You'll need tall sides on your container to prevent the wax from splattering when you turn your egg beater rapidly.

After the wax has completely melted, set it aside and allow it to cool until a thin "skin" appears on the surface.

When this film appears, begin the whipping process, either with an egg beater or a fork. (See Figure 74).

Figure 74

To make the whipped wax stick to the side of the candle, add one teaspoon of cornstarch per pound of wax; to attain a true whiteness, add one tablespoon of washing detergent (powder) per pound of wax. Both of these ingredients are added any time during the whipping process.

When the wax surface becomes fluffy, like divinity, it is time for its application. Daub it on your candle with a fork, spoon or gloved hand. If using a fork, do not press the frosting against the candle or you will create telltale fork marks. (See Figure 75).

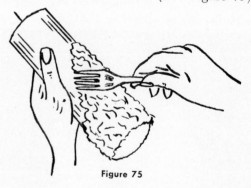

Figure 75

Repeated whippings are needed after the fluffy surface is used up each time. The faster you turn the egg beater, the fluffier your wax becomes.

After a candle has had the whipped wax applied, it may be desirable to dip it in a hot wax bath, or boiling water bath, to glaze the surface and smooth over any irregular lumps which may be objectionable.

With the above basic steps, anyone after a little practice can successfully apply wax to a candle. Many hobbyists also have their own individual hints and suggestions that are certainly worth passing on, and here are a few:

Hazel Clampitt of St. Paul, Minnesota: "For a light-colored frosting, beat the wax frothy; for a deep-colored frosting, beat the wax film very slightly."

Mary Pruden of Riverdale, New Jersey: "Put the whipped wax on with a fork for a rougher, snowier look. If you work on small trays or plates you won't have to handle them until the 'snow' is set."

Leona Harnden of Stillwater, Oklahoma: "I use paraffin with a melting point of 133° to 140° for whipping and whip the cooled wax till there's a layer of foam about two inches thick. Then, with a silver or stainless steel knife, I mix the foam with the liquid wax which makes it stick easier and prevents it from piling up in lumps. I like the color of the blank candle to show through the whipped cover to preserve the 'glow' quality of the candle. Occasionally, with a metal instrument, I have melted the whipped wax in a pattern, letting the color of the candle show through." (See Picture 18.)

Picture 18

Whether whipped wax is applied merely to cover blemishes on a candle surface or to create interesting and novel effects, its use enhances the beauty of most candles and offers the candle-maker ample opportunity for imaginative displays and works of art. (See Picture 19). The creation we will call a gold nugget candle bears close resemblance to a candle with gold nuggets im-

bedded at random in its surface. To create this effect, simply coat a candle with whipped wax, smooth over the jagged edges of wax by immersing the candle in hot water, and roll it on wax paper. Finally, paint the protruding portions of wax with gold paint. (See Group Picture IV, Page 80d.)

DRIP CANDLES

By "drip candles" we are not referring to candles which are treated to drip excessively or in different colors. We are talking about candles that give the *appearance* of having dripped profusely; that is, their sides are covered with "wax drips" and "runs," but they have been applied artificially.

Though the appearance of a dripping candle is quite attractive, the mess and bother tends to outweigh the home effect it creates. This is why many candle manufacturers strive to make their candles dripless. Therefore, we must create the drip effect under controlled circumstances to avoid a mess.

Melt and color a small amount of wax with which to create the drip effect. The color of this wax should be quite concentrated to assure its intensity on the candle surface.

When the temperature of the wax reaches approximately 165°, pour the wax into a small, spouted container, such as a measuring cup.

Position the candle at about a 70° angle on a piece of wax paper, which in turn is on a covering of newspaper.

Picture 19—Candles decorated with whipped wax created by Mrs. Clyde Jordan

Slowly pour the wax in spurts down the sides of the candle, beginning each "run" always from the top. Dribble out just a spoonful of wax occasionally so that the "run" will stop somewhere at the mid-portion of the candle. (See Figure 76.)

Figure 76

Revolve the candle after each "run" to keep the drip effect uniform on all sides and to provide each dripping an opportunity to cool after each application.

Complete the dripping process by setting the candle upright and dribbling the wax around the top edge of the candle and then around the wick. Be sure to coat the entire top surface of the candle to provide the illusion that the drips originated from the base of the wick.

When large "icicles" are desired, the dripping wax should be cooled until a "skin" forms on the surface before application.

Various eye-catching effects may be achieved with the drip effect, depending on the color scheme. Several harmonizing colors can be applied; one or two colors differing from the candle color; or a color identical with that of the candle. Whichever color scheme you desire, you can be assured of a candle display that will capture the attention and admiration of all who view it. (See Picture 20.)

Picture 20

BEESWAX CUTOUTS APPLICATION

Perhaps no other single item lends itself so well to candle decorating as sheet beeswax. Its characteristics are ideal for candles —colorful, pliable, easy to cut out and simple to attach. If you've worked with beeswax sheets you are well aware of these attributes, but if not, a brief explanation will prove worthwhile.

Normally sheet beeswax, generally available in colored sheets approximately 8″ by 16″, is used for rolling candles of all shapes and sizes. This process is discussed at some length in another section. Here, however, we are talking about "cut outs" of the beeswax being attached to the sides of a large block candle as a means of decoration. Since it is a soft, pliable wax with a natural adhesive quality, glue is never needed to attach it to a candle; merely press it on and it'll conform to the contours of any candle, be it round, square, star or what have you.

All you need for this type of decorating is the desired color of the sheet beeswax and a cutting instrument, such as a scissors, knife or razor blade. If the design you want is relatively simple, merely cut it out directly from the beeswax. If the design is quite intricate, it would be beneficial to cut out a pattern first and then cut the beeswax from the pattern.

In applying the beeswax designs, there are two general techniques favored: either the whole surface of the beeswax is pressed on the candle as an applique; or a three-dimensional appearance can be created by affixing only a portion of the beeswax to the candle with the remaining portion extending out and away from the candle. For lack of a better description, we'll call the first technique the "complete press" method; the latter technique identified as the "three dimensional" method. Consider the complete press method first, since it is the most widely used of the two.

COMPLETE PRESS TECHNIQUE

Once you realize the decorating potential of sheet beeswax your imagination will run wild. Following are a few ideas we dreamed up, ranging from pressing or pinning beeswax over the entire candle to pressing on small cut outs to coincide with the occasion.

Wrap the entire candle in a sheet of beeswax. Apply the sheet loosely to determine the correct size; mark it, cut it, wrap it firmly around the candle, and press the edges together on the backside.

Press and pin, harmonizing colorful strips of beeswax onto a white candle. These strips are applied horizontally, vertically, or diagonally; any width you choose (See Group Picture III, Page 80c.) These strips may even be pressed vertically on the points

of a white star candle, providing each point with a different harmony in colors. Here's an idea for creating an Eastern Star candle: press and pin strips of green, red, blue, yellow and white beeswax on the five points of a large white star candle.

Once you have affixed the beeswax sheet or strips to your candle, go a step further. Glaze the entire candle with its beeswax surface to achieve a smoother, more finished appearance. One important point to remember here, however, is that the dipping wax must not be over 190° or the beeswax "covering" will melt away. Four or five quick dips at 15-second intervals will suffice.

Continuing with the Complete Press Technique you will discover numerous ways to use smaller beeswax cut outs to depict certain holidays and occasions. Such as:

Valentine's Day. Red hearts pressed onto a candle. (See Picture 79.)

St. Patrick's Day. Green four-leaf clovers pressed onto a white candle or white pipes pressed onto a green candle.

Christmas. Colorful bells, trees or ornaments pressed onto a pink candle.

Halloween. A black cat pressed onto an orange candle.

Picture 22

THE THREE-DIMENSIONAL TECHNIQUE

This method of applying beeswax cut-outs runs from the simple to the complex, depending upon how fancy and realistic you wish to make your beeswax attachment.

A simple three-dimensional effect is created by a flower, protruding from the side of the candle. (See Picture 22.) First, make cardboard patterns for the petals and leaves. Form the stem by cutting a ¼" strip of green beeswax, folding it over to give it body and rolling it back and forth under your hand on a flat surface to round it out. Press the stem onto the candle, affix the flower at the desired position and you will be amazed how realistic your flower will look.

A more complex three-dimensional effect is found in a grape cluster. Here the beeswax is not only cut out but remolded to appear as grapes. Cut out about 30 two-inch squares from a sheet of purple beeswax and soften the squares by warming them on a piece of cardboard placed over a warm radiator or in front of a warm register. (See Figure 77.) Knead each square to form a "tight" lump, working it well with your fingers to achieve maximum fusion. (See Figure 78.) Roll each lump between your palms, forming small spheres, or "grapes." (See Figure 79.) Cut out a grape leaf pattern and form your beeswax grape leaves, using three or four thicknesses of beeswax for each leaf. (See Figure 80.) Knead and press the surface of the leaves with your fingers until relatively smooth; groove in veins with a ballpoint pen, and shape to resemble the natural contour of grape leaves. Assemble the "grapes" on the candle, affix the "leaves" around the cluster, and your display will look good enough to eat. (See Figure 81 and Group Picture II, Page 80b.)

WAX-PAINTED CANDLES

Some of the most beautiful candles have been those decorated with wax-painted scenes, flowers and designs. This takes much time and effort and a certain amount of

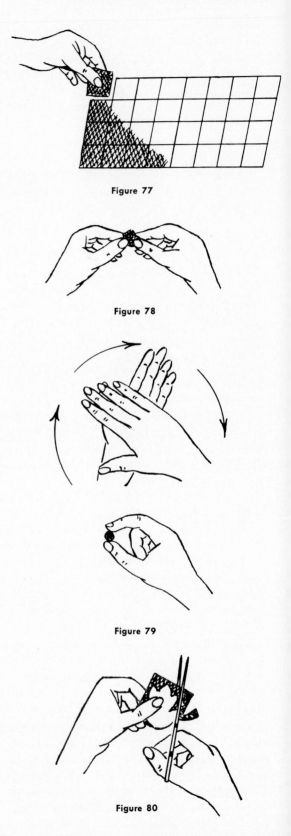

Figure 77

Figure 78

Figure 79

Figure 80

Figure 81

Figure 82

skill, but the result of the completed candle is reward enough. Such candles are rarely seen in the candle section of your local department store, for there is no way large candle companies can produce these what with the high labor costs and mass production methods being what they are. Such creations may be made only by the individual who has the patience, skill and know-how. So let's proceed to the "know-how" of wax-painted candles.

There are actually two methods of wax-painting; either with a brush or with a crayon. Most hobbyists prefer the brush method because of its greater versatility. The brush method involves more preparation, however, so we'll start with the simpler crayon method and proceed to the more complex method of brushing.

CRAYON METHOD

It is recognized that crayons should not be used for coloring candle wax, but they are quite suitable for our decorating technique. Mary Pruden of Riverdale, New Jersey, offers this excellent tip for those interested in the crayon method: "Want to write 'Happy Birthday' or someone's name or other greeting on a candle? In a small flame, heat the tip of a wax crayon to the melting point and write. (See Figure 82.) This cools very fast so it will have to be reheated after each stroke. The possibilities here are endless. Besides writing, you can make little sketches

and tell a story with little 'stick' men. By varying the pressure of the crayon you can achieve the effect of an oil painting. This is how white birch log candles are made, by drawing on the lines of the bark with black and brown crayons."

BRUSH METHOD

The old saying, "practice makes perfect," certainly applies to the brush method. Mrs. R. H. Liska of St. Marys, Ohio, sent us a sample of her work, with a note stating: "I have been trying for several years to teach myself to paint with wax the same as you would use oil paints and I hope you think my efforts have paid off." The picture of Mrs. Liska's hurricane candle in Group Picture II, Page 80b, is testimony enough that her efforts definitely have paid off.

It is often the little techniques and methods that differentiate the artist from the amateur. These techniques can even vary among the artists, depending upon the individual tastes of each.

Sketch a design on your candle by first drawing it on a piece of tracing paper. Next, turn the paper over and trace over the design with a soft lead pencil. Place the sketch on the candle, with the soft lead side next to the wax, and trace over the original sketch again with the pointed end of a knitting needle. This provides a good outline.

Prepare your wax colors for painting by mixing approximately four parts of clear wax to one part of a concentrated coloring, such as color crayons or regular candle wax coloring. This combination assures a smooth flow of the colored wax while painting.

Melt the colors in small containers (metal bottle caps, egg poaching pans, children's muffin tins, hand-made aluminum foil boxes, etc.) placed in a pan of hot water over slow heat. An alcohol burner is very suitable. Above the flame a frame may be installed in which a shallow pan of water is placed to provide slow and constant heat.

Different shades of the same color are easily obtained from the same "pan." The lightest shade is on the surface of your melted wax, while the darker shade is at the bottom. For a very dark shade, press the concentrated coloring against the side of the "pan" and dip your brush into it as it begins to melt. (See Picture 23.)

Picture 23

When your painting is completed you will want your brushes thoroughly cleaned. To do this, place them in boiling water for a few seconds, wipe them in a cleansing tissue, and dip in gasoline. This will remove any remaining wax.

WAX FLOWER APPLICATION

Few decorations go so well on a candle as hand-made wax flowers. They not only enhance the beauty of the candle, but they display the personal touch and artistic talents of the creator. Mrs. Leslie Townsend of St. Louis, Missouri, who has made numerous candles for all occasions, testifies to this: "I made pastel-colored six-pointed candles and put waxed flowers and leaves in the grooves around the base. They sold like hot cakes for showers and parties."

A book could be written on this method of decorating. For instance, they can be made from wax alone or devised from artificial or real flowers dipped in wax. To go further, flowers made solely of wax can be either hand-molded by one of numerous techniques, or formed in a mold at the time of pouring, of which there are several types. To save confusion, we'll cover each method individually, beginning with the wax flowers.

FLOWERS MADE FROM WAX

Formed from wax sheets. If you want to form a flower—say, a rose with the inner petals a darker shade than the outer petals— it is desirable to melt wax in small containers of various shades to acquire realistic coloring of your finished flower. When the desired shades have been attained, your next step is to form thin, dough-like sheets of wax via one of two methods. One method is to pour a thin layer of wax on the surface of hot water. The alternate, more widely-used method, is to pour a thin layer of wax from each container onto either a plate or cookie sheet that has been lightly oiled. A wide piece of heavy wax paper will also do (See Figure 83).

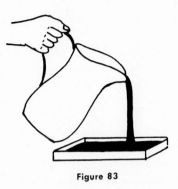

Figure 83

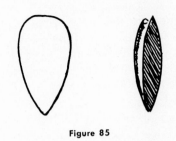

Figure 85

In both methods let the layers of wax cool until they are hard enough to withdraw with a knife or spatula, yet pliable enough to permit shaping by hand. At this point, cut out the petals with a paring knife, cutting several at one time so that each petal has a chance to thoroughly cool, thereby making them easier to handle (See Figure 84).

three petals of the same color are dipped and placed along the bud and shaped. Follow with larger petals and lighter shades until you are done (See Figure 86).

Figure 86

Figure 84

After the flower is assembled, its base may be dipped in dark green wax for added realism (See Figure 87). To attach the flower, take a heated knitting needle and melt out a hole in the candle. Weld the flower to the candle with the hot melted wax.

When cutting out the petals, or any wax figure, it is best to have a pattern ready beforehand. For perfection, use real petals or leaves, the shapes of which may be transferred to paper or cardboard prior to application on the wax layers to provide easier handling and continued use. One quick hint —should the wax sheets become too cold and rigid to cut and shape, soften them by immersing in warm water.

Next comes the assembly. Starting with the smaller and darker shades, the petal is dipped into its respective hot wax container to give it a smoother finish and then shaped to form a bud (See Figure 85). Two or

Figure 87

The above method of forming and anchoring wax flowers has been used and recommended by Elizabeth Dickie of Nova Scotia. Other hobbyists and professionals use basically the same technique.

A common practice in fastening wax pieces together is to use a hot spoon at the point of junction, in much the same manner as Mrs. Dickie uses her knitting needle. Merely lay the candle on its side, touch the back of a hot spoon to the spot desired, and place your small wax figure quickly in this puddle of melted wax.

Another method widely used could be classified as "welding." Here's how: Hold the small figure against the candle and with a clean, hot knife touch the point of junction at the top. Continue to "weld" the wax figure to the candle by touching the heated knife against all sides of the junction. Rotate the candle as you progress so that the welding is always being performed at the top, thus preventing dripping and assuring a better bond.

Another variation is to dip the back side of the figure into hot wax and press it quickly against the candle. To assure a stronger bond, create a puddle of wax on the candle in which to press the wax figure. Incidentally, regardless of the bonding method you use, don't move the figure once it has been stuck to the candle or the bond will be destroyed.

Mrs. R. J. Davis, of Albany, Oregon, offers this method for keeping the wax layers pliable: "Take a box, affix a light bulb in it (low watt), and place a glass to fit the box on top. It should also fit a built-up edge of wood around the edge so that when cooled wax is poured on the glass, it will not run out or off the sides. There will be just enough heat through the glass to maintain the right temperature, thus permitting molding the wax any design desired until finished" (See Figure 88).

Mrs. Leona Harnden, of Stillwater, Oklahoma, keeps her wax warm and pliable for molding purposes by using a similar method. She pours the wax into a pyrex plate, which is then placed over a box with a light inside. She also has a very effective method of creating and attaching wax flowers, as related here in her own description of creating a poinsettia display: "I molded a pink candle in a large round straight mold and covered it with a layer of whipped wax. I melted a $\frac{3}{16}''$ thickness of pink wax in a pyrex plate. When it had solidified, but was still soft enough to be cut with a pin, I cut out poinsettia-shaped petals. With a tiny spatula, I lifted the petals and placed them on the candle, one at a time, pressing them down against the whipped wax. I have been using a poinsettia pattern cut from a Christmas card and when it is pressed against the firm but soft wax, the veins of the petals leave their impression in the wax. I cut a narrow strip to use for the stem, or with a hot instrument melt a valley and put melted pink wax for the stem. Green wax can also be used. I have a pattern taken from a poinsettia leaf. When the leaves are in place and the candle has had time to be thoroughly cooled, I dip it in the glaze vat and then paint the edges of the leaves with silver paint" (See Pictures 15 and 57).

Mrs. C. C. Dunkle, of Pinehurst, Idaho, suggests her method for obtaining thin petals that are desirable with any flowers: "When the wax is the proper consistency to mold, place a small piece between two sheets of wax paper and roll very thin with a rolling pin. To make small rose buds, I then cut small heart-shaped pieces and form together to resemble buds. For stamens I use artificial ones tied with a stem wire and dipped in wax. Punch a hole in the center of the flower, insert the stamen and paint melted wax, previously used for the inner portion of the flower, around the base of the stamen."

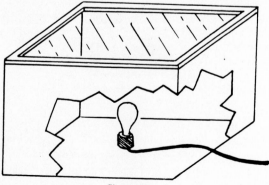

Figure 88

One problem which is inherent with wax flowers is the brittleness of the petals. Mrs. E. E. Horne, of Denver, Colorado, has solved this problem nicely: "After the wax layer has cooled for a minute or two, I place a sheet of crepe paper over it and pour another thin layer of wax over this. I mark the petals before the wax gets real cold and then warm the wax sheets in hot water and cut out the petals with scissors. The inner layer of crepe paper prevents the leaves from breaking."

An alternate method of coloring your flowers would be to paint them with melted colored wax or wax paints (available from either Lumi Lite Candle Co., Zanesville, Ohio, or the Pourette Mfg. Co.) Either method offers a greater range of colors and eliminates the necessity of making the petals various shades when pouring.

Wax leaves are made the same way as the petals. Veins are easily attained by pressing them in with a corsage pin while the wax is still soft. It is also very easy to paint the leaves and stems directly on the candle after the flowers are placed in the desired position. The latter method, however, does not give the leaves the depth or extend out as they would were they hand-molded, but by repeated brushings with a very small brush and liquid green wax, an effect closely resembling three dimensions is acquired.

Another way to creat small petals or leaves very rapidly is to pour the wax into a spoon and slide the wax out after it has cooled.

Wax flowers formed with balloons. Here's another way to create wax flowers:

Take a round balloon, fill it with cold water and tie or clamp the neck closed (See Figure 89). Melt wax of the desired color

Figure 89

Figure 90

Figure 91

Figure 92

Figure 93

Figure 94

until the temperature reaches approximately 180°. Dip the balloon into the wax eight to 12 times, depending upon the thickness of the wax coating desired (See Figure 90). Each dip should be at intervals of about five to 10 seconds to allow for a proper "setting-up" period. After the final dip, open the neck, pour out the water and withdraw the balloon (See Figure 91). You now have a hollow round "shell" of wax with which to work in molding flower petals. To keep this shell pliable while forming, fill the interior with hot water (See Figure 92).

In order to peel back the "petals," it is necessary to cut four or five slits down the sides of the shell from the opening (See Figure 93). From this point on, your own creative talents will guide you in properly shaping the petals.

By nestling smaller "shells" together successively, you can create realistic flowers for use in a number of ways. They can be attached to a candle, floated in water, or merely displayed in a table setting or on a mantel arrangement. If you want to make a candle from the flower, merely imbed a votive glass in the center and set a votive candle in for burning (See Figure 94).

Wax flowers formed with bowl. A small bowl can be used to form a flower, particularly a water lily. Cut out a number of hearts from a layer of soft wax and arrange them around the inside edge of the bowl so that their sides overlap and their points are at the bottom (See Figure 95). Pour wax of the same color into the bowl until it covers the overlapping edges of the hearts (See Figure 96). When this wax has cooled, pour a small dab of yellow wax into the center, let it set

for a few minutes, and sprinkle bits of black crayon on it to resemble the stigma of the flower (See Figure 97).

Upon removal from the bowl, the "petals" might require added forming. Simply submerge the flower in hot water, softening the wax and permitting easy shaping. If you prefer converting a wax flower into a candle, place a small votive glass and candle in the center and you'll have a unique candle that will last indefinitely (See Figure 97-A).

Wax flowers formed with molds. By far the easiest way of creating wax flowers is with flower molds. These molds are made of plastic and normally come in sheets containing a wide selection. They can be purchased from Wilton Enterprises, Inc., Chicago, or Pourette Mfg. Co.

Since the shape and feature of the "flowers" are built into the mold, no carving, shaping or reforming is necessary. For added realism, however, it is suggested that these wax flowers be painted with colored wax or wax paint before being anchored to a candle.

ARTIFICIAL FLOWERS DIPPED IN WAX

If you know how to create artificial flowers from such material as crepe paper or wood fibre, then you are indeed fortunate. If you don't know how and want to learn, courses in flower-making are usually offered periodically by local hobby or artificial flower supply shops. You can, of course, purchase ready-made wood fibre flowers or acquire them as Mary Pruden suggests: "Faded flowers from the millinery department have a soft pastel effect when waxed.

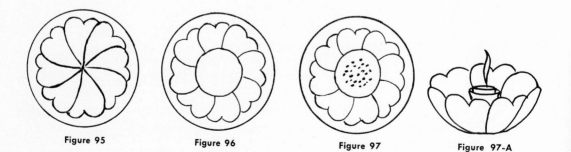

Figure 95   Figure 96   Figure 97   Figure 97-A

You can often get these very cheaply when faded window displays are dismantled. Get to know a few window dressers in your home town; they'll tip you off when these things are available."

Such creations can be used for numerous things besides candle decorations, but for purposes of this book, it is best that we stick to how they lend themselves to candles.

Waxing artificial flowers is relatively easier than going through the involved process of creating flowers solely from wax. Mrs. John Tomaski of Prosser, Washington, tells us how she makes candles for wedding tables and parties: "I dip small pastel colored artificial flowers and their leaves into melted clear wax two times, then fasten a garland to the candle with small pins, taking a drop of warm wax on a toothpick and transferring it to the head of the pin to conceal it."

Leaves are also made out of bleached muslin. Cut out leaf shape; put in pan of liquid wax; fish out with a fork and cool on wax paper. Re-dip until thick enough, and shape while warm.

Even leaves cut from wax paper and dipped repeatedly in liquid wax have been used with very satisfactory results.

WAXING REAL FLOWERS

In many instances you can go directly to Mother Nature for flowers and leaves that lend themselves to the liquid wax dipping process. This preserves them for a period of about two weeks, at the same time giving them the rigidity and firmness needed for attaching to a candle.

Because flowers and leaves are normally much more delicate than their artificial counterparts, a few important facts must be kept in mind if you are to have any success. Use only freshly cut flowers and do not attempt to dip any more than one blossom or spray at a time. Dip them alternately into wax at about 150° and ice-cold water approximately five times. Allow the waxed flower to cool by laying flat on a piece of wax paper.

WAX FIGURE APPLICATION

You can do just about anything with wax; if you have any doubts, this section should convince you. If you wish to adorn your candle with wax figures there is absolutely no limit to the size, shape, or color.

Cookie cutters come in numerous shapes that can be used to press out small wax figures from a sheet of warm wax. Other figures can be copied from magazines or cards and outlined on wax sheets with either a knife or pin. Free hand-drawing patterns may be drawn and cut out to be used as a guide for outlining in wax any shape desired.

Small molds used in baking or candymaking are ideal for forming wax figures. Wiltons and Pourette, previously mentioned as having flower molds, have mold sets available containing a variety of figures (See Pictures 25, 26).

In some instances you may wish to apply a relatively large flat wax figure on a round or oval candle, but prefer that the figure fit the round contours of the candle surface rather than protruding out on a tangent. In other words, the wax figure must be *bent* to coincide with the shape of the candle, an almost impossible accomplishment if you don't know how to go about it. Here is an effective method we found to be extremely simple.

Submerge the figure in a container filled with hot tap water for a few minutes until pliable.

Instead of pressing the pliable figure directly on to the candle, first apply it against the candle mold, thus eliminating the possibility of damaging the candle in the process. To maintain the pliability of wax figure throughout the forming process it is advantageous to warm your mold beforehand. This is best accomplished by plugging up the wick hole, filling the mold with hot water and allowing it to set for approximately one minute until the mold is warmed.

Picture 25

Picture 26

Figure 98

With the mold now warmed, slowly press the wax figure upside down against its surface until the backside conforms to the mold surface (See Figure 98).

Pour out the hot water, refill with cold water and continue holding the figure against the mold until it hardens again.

With the figure now rounded to fit the candle's contour, it may be affixed to the candle with wax weld or melted wax and a most professional candle is the result (See Picture 27).

It definitely pays to keep your eyes open for any item that can be used in molding wax figures. You'll find them almost anywhere, even in your own home. Mrs. Bernard Otness of Prosser, Washington, even figured out a way of using old flash bulbs in her candle decorating. She says: "We took burned white flash bulbs #5, wired each with heavy wire, and taped with corsage tape in a color to blend with the colored wax to be used. Then we dipped the bulbs one at a time in warm, colored wax until the

Picture 28

bulb became the same color as the candle. This takes from seven to ten dippings—cooling between times—then forming a cluster of seven to eleven waxed grapes for a stunning combination. At Christmas I made several in white wax to match three white candles and used them singly with gold balls the same size for an outstanding mantel decoration."

Novel figures can even be made from such unrelated items as drinking glasses. Freeman Hover of Canon City, Colorado, writes: "I have found that wax bells, used for adorning Christmas candles or for wedding candles, can be made very simply by pouring hot wax into a wine glass and let it harden. Here's how it's done (See Figure 99). Fill the wine glass with liquid wax, after having first pre-heated the glass by running hot water over the exterior. Allow the wax to set until a layer of wax approximately 3/16″ thick forms on the sides and top. At this point cut out the top layer as you would a hurricane candle and pour out the center,

Picture 27

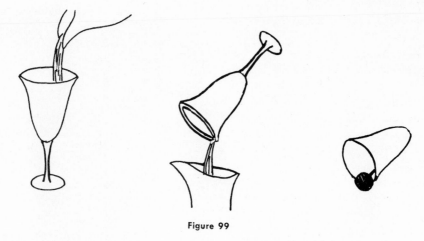

Figure 99

leaving a thick coating of wax on the inside of the glass. Cool this coating completely before removing from the wine glass. The bell clapper can be improvised by tying a wired ornamental ball to the inside, and your bell is complete. If desired, it may be trimmed with glitter, sequins and the like" (See Picture 28).

A smaller bell may be made out of a jigger rather than a wine glass. When using these small glasses it is not necessary to pour out the center liquid wax as the natural settling "well" provides a cavity. These small bells, when placed around the candle base, constitute an exceptionally attractive display and a real conversation piece.

Still another extremely effective method of using wax figures for candle decorating is with molded wax grapes. Mrs. D. O. Pearson of Burlington, Washington, writes that such candles won for her Garden Club a state award at the Garden Club Christmas Exhibit. "A large full bunch of wax grapes made life-size and dipped in three shades of wax to harmonize with the candles, were first wired to the candle with fine wire wrapped with parafilm colored the same as the candles. Curlicues and artificial leaves were then applied providing the whole display with a three-dimensional look."

The following brief instruction will enable you to create your own grapes. Before commencing with the actual "production" of grapes, obtain the following items from your local florist: floral wire, floral tape, spiral wire or curlicues, and grape leaves. Wrap each wire with floral tape and the grape "stems" are ready to use. Now proceed with the actual creating of the grapes.

Melt soft wax (125-130° melting point) and color desired grape color.

When the wax temperature approaches 170°, pour into shallow tray or pan a thickness of approximately ¾" deep.

Let this wax set at room temperature for about three hours, at which time it should be ready to "work."

With a watermelon-ball scoop or measuring spoon, dip out wax balls and work the wax between the palms of your hands until the surface is smooth (See Figure 79).

While wax "balls" are still soft, insert into each one a "stem"; the wire covered with floral tape.

To acquire a sheen on each grape give each one a quick dip into melted wax colored the same as the grapes and hold upright to prevent excess wax from forming a drop on the outer extremity.

Form your grape cluster by binding together with the floral tape, adding one grape at a time for the proper effect (See Figure 103).

Attach two or three spiral wires (curlicues) into the cluster and work in two or three grape leaves at the top (See Figure 104).

The completed grape cluster is then laid

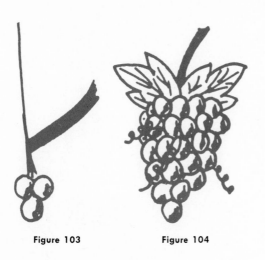

Figure 103   Figure 104

The first requirement is to make or buy a tall plain candle with a diameter ranging from 1″ to 3″. Place it in a bowl (about 5″ diameter) and pour a layer of wax over the base of the bowl to secure the candle to the bowl (See Figure 105). Melt additional wax of a color that will harmonize with the color of your candle and pour it into the bowl at 165° (See Figure 106). Pour only enough wax to bring the level up to about an inch. Immediately after pouring submerge the whole assembly—candle, bowl and liquid wax—into a deep container of tepid water. It should hold enough water to permit the complete submersion of candle and bowl. As the candle is lowered into the water, the liquid wax, being lighter than water, rises to the surface, clinging to the sides of the candle and hardening at the same time. This forms a spiral effect by turning the candle slowly as it is lowered into the water (See Figure 107). Incidentally, wear a glove while lowering the candle in case the liquid wax clings to your hand and candle.

at the base of the candle, or attached to the side of the candle with the aid of half pins —or wired on as previously mentioned (See Picture 29).

MOLTEN BASE WATER DIP

While this candle is unique and unusual, it is relatively simple to make (See Picture 30). The interesting thing about creating these candles is that no two look alike.

Numerous bizarre shapes are attained by this process, yet little can be done to create one to exact specifications. You will also discover that if the wax is too hot or too cold undesired effects occur. For instance, if the

Picture 29

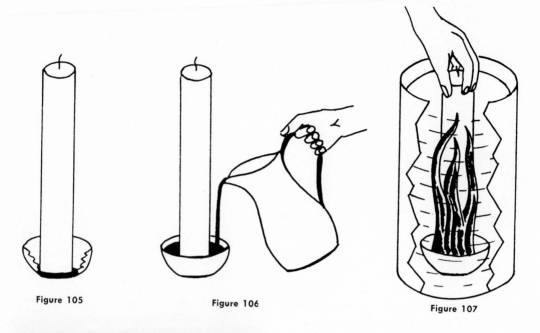

Figure 105   Figure 106   Figure 107

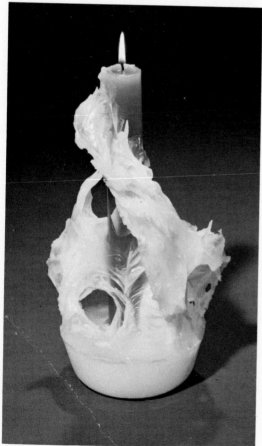

Picture 30

wax temperature exceeds 165° the wax may cover the candle like a wrinkled sleeve, or if below 165°, the wax will rise only a few inches above the bowl and refuse to cling to the candle.

Another popular feature of this candle is the built-in base derived from the hardened wax remaining in the bowl. When the bowl is removed the remaining wax assumes the shape of the bowl, providing a wide solid base for the candle.

FLOATING CANDLES

For a novel centerpiece try a table arrangement featuring floating candles. Mrs. Frank Rittmueller of Frankenmuth, Michigan, writes: "Individual jello molds, especially the star mold, make very good floating candles. I usually trim them with a border of glitter or the tiny star sequins (attached with pins) purchased at the dime store" (See Figure 108).

To assure a light-weight candle (necessary for floating candles) press whipped wax into the mold. The wick is pressed into the wax at the same time, or you may prefer inserting a birthday candle into the wax.

Figure 108

A large floating candle is made in much the same fashion as a hurricane candle. Simply make a wax shell from a shallow bowl and place a votive candle in the center to provide the light. Mrs. Calvin Jones of Houston, Texas, makes beautiful candles using this method. She colors the votive candles to harmonize with the color of the "shell" by dipping the candle into the melted wax that has been poured out of the bowl. The votive candle is placed in the center of the wax shell, either before the shell has hardened completely or afterwards. "When the candle has burned down, it can be replaced over and over again, because the shell will last indefinitely," adds Mrs. Jones.

Decorating Techniques Without Wax

GLITTER AND GLITTER CEMENT

There is no end to the attractive designs that can be concocted when you sit down before a candle with a few decorations, some cement, glitter and a little imagination.

Anyone who has used glitter for decorating candles will agree that there is no more breath-taking combination.

Glitter is so simple to apply and comes in such a variety of colors that there's little wonder why candle-makers use it so often. It can be applied two ways: (1) *unrestricted* —over the whole candle; (2) *restricted*—on certain spots only. The *unrestricted* technique—how it is done and where it is used —will be described first.

When applying glitter to the whole candle you must first prepare the candle surface to enable the glitter to stick. A simple but very effective way is to spray glitter cement (in a spray can) over the entire candle just prior to sprinkling on the glitter (See Figure 109-A). Another way is to immerse the candle in a dipping vat of hot wax, commonly referred to as "glazing" a candle, and while the wax is still tacky sprinkle on the glitter (See Fig. 109-B).

The *unrestricted* technique can be used on a candle of any shape or color and the glitter may be one color or many. Mrs. Nellie Thacker of Vernonia, Oregon, states: "I

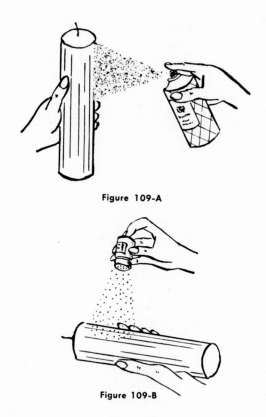

Figure 109-A

Figure 109-B

sprayed most of mine this year with glitter cement, sprinkled glitter on them, and they were beautiful."

A third way of applying glitter is to spray the plain candle first with a colored paint. While the paint is still wet, sprinkle on a harmonizing shade of glitter. Mrs. Jay Bottger of Spokane, Washington, uses this technique and found the following combination particularly attractive: "Any colored candle covered with copper metallic paint sprinkled with blue glitter" (See Picture 31).

Picture 31

When using the *restricted* method, there is no limit to what can be accomplished. Since this method prohibits glitter from adhering to the whole candle and on certain areas only, a brush must be used to apply the glitter cement precisely where you want the glitter to stick. Incidentally, nail polish can also be used to cement glitter to wax.

After the glitter has been "dusted" on, it is necessary to tap the candle on your work-ing area to remove excess glitter that tends to cling to the wax. If unwanted glitter still persists, brush it off with a dry brush.

The shooting star candle (See Group Picture I, Page 80a) and the snowflake candle (See Group Picture III, Page 80c) are examples of what can be accomplished with some glitter, glitter cement and star sequins. For the shooting stars, merely pin on the stars, brush a tail with glitter cement, and sprinkle on the glitter. For the colorful snowflakes, sprinkle on the glitter over lines daubed with glitter cement.

When using glitter always work over a newspaper or similiar covering so that the excess glitter may be saved. Simply make a crease in the covering, shake the excess glitter into the trough, and pour it into your glitter bottle.

Mrs. Charles Russell of New Brighton, Minnesota, has made and sold several candles using this restricted technique. Her instructions are simple to follow. "With a six-pointed star candle, rough the surface on one side of each point with sandpaper, apply cement over this, sprinkle on the glitter and remove the excess. Very effective color combinations are silver glitter on a red candle, or gold glitter on a white candle. The glitter may be applied in three different styles" (See Figure 111).

Should you desire to create intricate designs, sketches, letters or numbers for your candle, a relatively new product will assist you. It's called "Glitter Magic" or "Glitter Glue" and is nothing more than a pre-mixture of glitter and glitter cement; comes in a squeeze tube. All you have to do is squeeze the tube and out comes a thin line

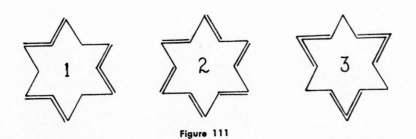

Figure 111

of glitter, making it relatively simple to "draw" definite lines without blotches or smudges. Numerous colors are available, so if you're artistic, there're numerous possibilities for clever and colorful designs (See Picture 32).

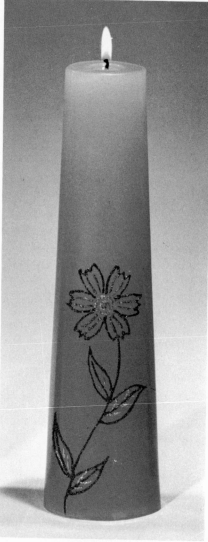

Picture 32

Guide method. Variations of this method may be devised, but a simple guide for lettering is shown here. Merely cut a slot in a piece of paper corresponding to the height you want the letters on the candle to be. Print or write just above the slot a duplicate of the lettering as a guide to proper spacing. Copy these letters directly on the candle in the slot to get uniform letters (See Figure 112).

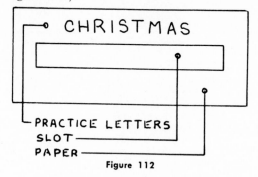

Figure 112

Pattern method. First, draw the design you want on paper to fit over the candle. Place the paper design on the candle where it is to be duplicated; either pin-prick through the design on to the candle or press on the design with a ballpoint pen (See Figure 113). Using the pin-pricks as a guide, apply the cement and dust with glitter. That's all there is to it.

Figure 113

Whether you use the newer glitter-tube method or the conventional glitter and glitter-cement technique, it isn't advisable to apply the glitter freehand—a mistake cannot be erased. Consequently, we suggest one of the following methods to assure a perfect creation on the first attempt.

Stencil method. Again draw the desired figure on a paper, but this time cut out the design, leaving a stencil. Place the stencil over the candle, apply the cement, dust with glitter and your candle is beautifully decorated.

TRANSFERS AND DECALS

Roth Rineglas Transfers and Meyercord Decals offer you a whole new approach to candle decorating. They are extremely simple to apply and will easily stick on a candle providing the surface is non-porous.

The Rineglas Transfers consist normally of the following groups: (1) designs and figures of one color—gold, silver or copper; (2) leaves and ferns of one color—green, tan or gold; (3) plain colored sheets—available in several colors. With the large selection of designs available, you have a limitless range of custom-decorating possibilities. Even the plain-colored sheets offer a variety of effects through clever positioning and cutting. Keep in mind that one color can be transferred over another, each transparent color blending with the underlying one, producing sparkling intermediate colors (See Picture 36). One may also create a novel effect by placing a designed transfer over a colored transfer (See Pictures 37, 38).

The Meyercord Decals consist largely of colorful figures and scenes which cannot help but add life and interest to your candles. They are more conventional and realistic than the Rineglas Transfers; therefore, are used where a definite picture or scene is desired, rather than an abstract effect.

Picture 36

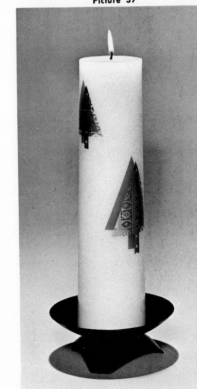

Picture 37

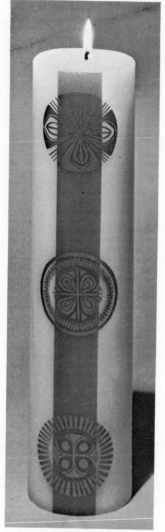

Picture 38

Mrs. F. O. Ware of Minneapolis, Minnesota, writes us that she has made several interesting candles with the help of the Meyercord Decals. "I find that gold and black decals on plain white candles are particularly effective," she adds (See Picture 39).

A semi-obscure effect may be acquired by dipping the completed candle into hot wax. This thin wax coating seems to add quality to the candle. It also provides excellent protection against excessive handling.

PAINTED CANDLES

Certain paints will stick to wax where others only "bead up" without covering the surface. If you try your hand at painting candles, be sure to use a paint that will adhere to wax, such as those provided by the Lumi Lite Candle Company and Pourette Mfg. Co. that have been developed specifically for application on wax (See Picture 40 and Group Picture I, Page 80a.)

There are, of course, two main methods of applying paint—by *spraying* or *brushing*. An excellent spray paint is chromatone. It comes in a variety of colors. Mrs. Delbert Adamson of Hays, Kansas, offers several suggestions for the application of spray paint: "I spatter-spray the bottom three-quarters of the candle with silver, gold or bronze. Working quickly, so the paint will still be wet, I sprinkle glitter over the wet paint. This is

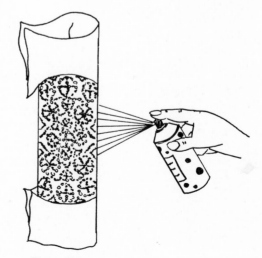

Figure 114

Picture 39

especially pretty on dark candles and bright red ones. However, I sprayed a pure white candle with gold—glittered the paint with gold—used a white whipped wax snow base, which I also sprinkled with gold glitter, and used all gold ornaments on the base. The result was just beautiful."

Another idea for a bizarre effect, spray the paint through a paper lace doily (See Figure 114). To explain this one further, wrap a large lace doily around an oval or three-inch round candle, adhering it to the candle with scotch tape. Cover all parts of the candle-surface surrounding the doily with paper so that the only wax surface exposed is that showing through the doily pattern. Do not use half-pins to secure the doily or the paper to the candle unless necessary, for the resulting pin marks detract from its beauty. When your "covering" has been completed, spray the candle any color you desire; it normally takes two or three coats to acquire a good coverage. After the paint has thoroughly dried, remove the doily and paper—and you have a beautiful candle much like that shown in Picture 41.

Painting designs, scenes or figures on a candle with a brush needs no explanation. Some innovations have been devised by individual candle-making enthusiasts, however, that are worth mentioning. For instance, if you want to subdue the bright

Picture 40

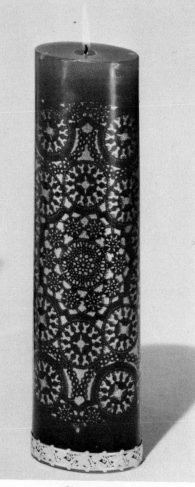

Picture 41

paint colors on your candle, dip the entire candle into liquid wax (180°), providing a richer appearance to your artistry. You might also first carve a design or figure on your candle with a linoleum carver, then paint in the grooves to "bring out" the design more clearly.

For a spectacular display achieved with paints, try the paint swirl technique, a method devised by Mrs. Helen Agoa of Fort Lawton, Washington. Fill a deep cylinder with just enough warm water so that you can submerge your candle the entire length without overflowing. Spoon about four spoonfuls of paint on the surface of the water, being careful to keep the paint floating. If the paint is dropped or poured onto

the surface it will break the tension of the water and undesirably sink. After the paint has been "applied" to the water surface, set it in a slight swirling motion with a stick. While the paint is swirling about the surface, lower your candle into the water by holding on to the wick—and you have a uniquely-painted candle (See Picture 43 and Group Picture II, Page 80b).

ARTIFICIAL FLOWERS, FRUITS, FOLIAGE

If you have access to such artificial accessories, your candle decorating becomes relatively simple. Modern techniques have made the imitations so real that their lasting qualities have sometimes made them

Picture 43

Picture 44

more desirable to use than their real coun-
terpart. Their wire stem also assists the candle-maker immensely in combining and
securing situations.

Since there is no limit to the various ways
these accessories are used, we won't attempt
a lengthy discourse on their application. A
few candles using artificial fruit and flowers
and so forth are shown in Pictures 44, 45,
46, 47, 57 and in Group Picture II, Page 80b.
Mrs. Helen Medin of Seattle, Washington,
uses artificial flowers on all her candles. "I
can't make them fast enough to meet the
demand," she enthuses. Two of Mrs. Medin's
candles are shown in Group Picture IV,
Page 80d.

Picture 45

Picture 46

Picture 47—Candles decorated with artificial flowers
created by Mrs. Helen Medin

AT THE JEWELRY COUNTER

Mary Pruden writes: "Make friends with the girl at the dime store jewelry counter. (Give her a pretty candle!) She will save broken jewelry for you. If you are nice to the manager, you can get a shoe box full for about a dollar. You'll have enough loose stones, pearls, beads, chain, odd earrings, pinless pins, broken bracelets and necklaces to keep you going all year. The best time to pick up this little bargain is just after they have cleaned up after the holidays."

This is excellent advice, another example of how being a little resourceful will pay off. Mrs. Pruden also has a word of advice for women who might have an obsolete piece of jewelry lying around the house: "If you lose one of your glamorous costume earrings, don't throw away its mate! Use it as the center of an ornate medallion on a fat, round, oval cone or square candle. Snip off the earwire with wire cutters so it will lie flat. Glue it in the center of a large gold foil medallion and surround it with sequins and rhinestones and pearls in a gaudy baroque effect; frame the whole thing with whipped wax. In this case, I usually omit glitter—it detracts from the central medallion. A costume jewelry bracelet or necklace with a broken or missing catch can be taken apart and used the same way, or fastened around the candle in one piece."

Mrs. Bernice Kellis of Vancouver, Washington, suggests making a Baby Shower Candle with jewelry: "Pour a three-inch square white candle. Attach blue or pink nylon velvet ribbon around the bottom with half pins and pearls or beads and sequins. Cover entire candle with diamond dust glitter. Apply rhinestones, using a large blue one in the center and smaller clear ones placed above and below."

With a little imagination, jewelry, pins or beads and a large block candle, you can create a decorative candle surpassing any you might find in a candle shop. Our purpose here is to bring to your attention the decorative possibilities of jewelry; how you apply it is left up to you.

SEQUINS

Sequins are particularly suited for candle decorating. They come in numerous designs and are very easy to apply. Simply decide on a candle design or pattern and apply the sequins with small pins. They can also be used to supplement other decorations, such as glitter, decoupage and whipped wax (Pictures 49 and 50 offer ideas in which sequins can be used, as does Figure 118).

CHRISTMAS BALLS AND BELLS

The very ornateness of these decorations makes them particularly suitable for the holiday season. Small balls or bells may be attached to the side of a candle; embedded into whipped wax about the base or tied on with ribbon, greens or other harmonizing decorations. In short, they are applied in numerous ways. Figure 119 provides a few ideas in which Christmas balls and bells

Picture 49

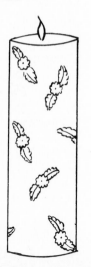

Figure 118

Picture 50

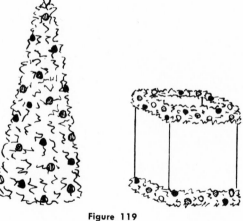

Figure 119

have been used to enhance the beauty of holiday candles.

A particularly attractive candle is one which utilizes Christmas balls of all sizes. Here's how: Stand a large candle, three to four inches in diameter, on a tray or mirror to form a portable base. Remove the wire hooks from an assortment of bright Christmas tree ornaments; hang the balls on pins that have been stuck into the candle at an angle. Place small balls at the top, large ones at the bottom. Pile evergreen boughs around the base of the candle and cover them with a colorful assortment of large balls to complete the arrangement (See Group Picture IV, Page 80d.)

GROUP PICTURE I

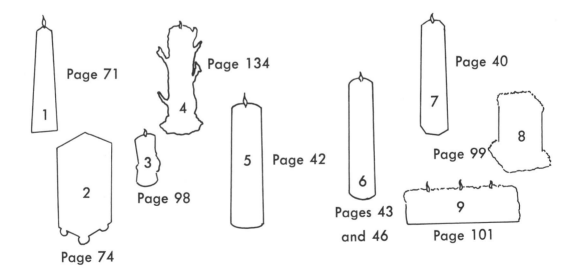

Page 71

1

Page 74

2

Page 134

4

Page 98

3

Page 42

5

Pages 43
and 46

6

Page 40

7

Page 99

Page 101

8

9

For directions on creating these candles refer to pages listed above.

80A

GROUP PICTURE II

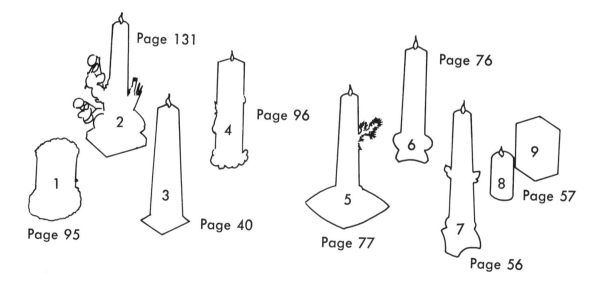

Page 131

Page 76

Page 96

2

4

Page 57

9

1

6

3

8

5

7

Page 95

Page 40

Page 77

Page 56

For directions on creating these candles refer to pages listed above.

GROUP PICTURE III

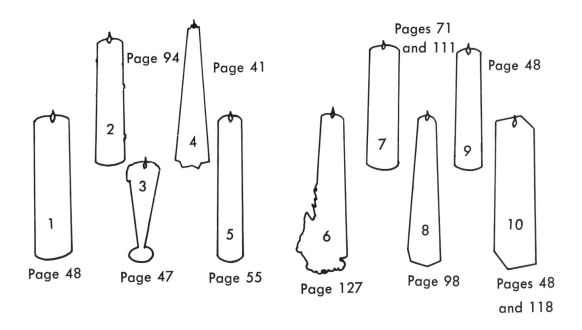

Page 94   Page 41

Pages 71 and 111   Page 48

2   4   7   9

3

1   5   6   8   10

Page 48   Page 47   Page 55

Page 127

Page 98

Pages 48 and 118

For directions on creating these candles refer to pages listed above.

GROUP PICTURE IV

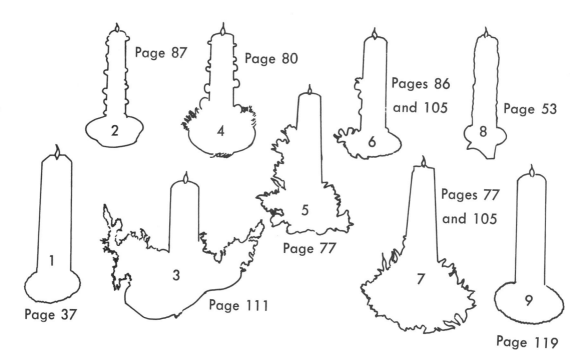

Page 87 — 2
Page 80 — 4
Pages 86 and 105 — 6
Page 53 — 8
Page 37 — 1
Page 111 — 3
Page 77 — 5
Pages 77 and 105 — 7
Page 119 — 9

For directions on creating these candles refer to pages listed above.

SEA SHELLS

Mrs. G. A. Culpepper of Las Cruces, New Mexico, writes: "For direct ornamentation, my favorite has been sea shells." Judging from numerous letters we have received from other candle crafters, it is apparent that sea shells are also the favorite of those who are fortunate enough to have access to them. Let's look at a few sea-shell ideas.

From Mrs. W. H. Dumeyer of Salisbury, Maryland: "A friend collects for me small sea shells, all shapes and sizes, in Florida each year. To preserve the lovely colors, I first wash them and then dip into cooking oil and dry with a paper towel. I then cluster a large amount of shell at the base of the candle until it drifts almost to the top, ending with a tiny shell. In among the shells are placed stones from old pieces of jewelry, touched off with sequins the color of the candle. This takes time because you must lay the candle down as you work so as not to move the shells while the glue is drying. It's one of the most popular candles with my customers at Christmas time" (See Picture 51).

From Elizabeth Dickie of Nova Scotia: "I place real bits of shells, sea urchins, sea mice, crab shells and anything native to this coastal area on a pale green hurricane. I then place some pale green plastic netting around the hurricane, anchoring it at the top and bottom with sequin pins. Then I dip just the edges into hot wax to cement the edges."

From Mrs. Raymond De Briae of Cathlamet, Washington: "First, I take a candle with a flat surface. Then I make flowers from sea shells. I use either gardenia, roses, violets, pansies, daisies or dogwood. All are made from shells and range from real small to two inches. I have made a spray of both one variety and a combination of several kinds of flowers. I use Bond cement and a little bit of cotton to secure the shell flower to the candle. For leaves, either large shells or small cloth or foil leaves are used. For Mother's Day, a gold or silver Mother is placed in the center of the spray. Finish

Picture 51

with blending braid at the bottom and glitter to match, if desired."

From Mrs. G. A. Culpepper of Las Cruces, New Mexico: "I use a rosy mauve tapered pyramid (flat sides work best). Small shells, pearls, bits of coral are glued to the candle about three-quarters of the way up. I use two sides, making the corner of the candle the focal point. I use a lavender sea fan lightly glittered as a background for the candle and spike the whole arrangement onto a piece of driftwood" (See Figure 120).

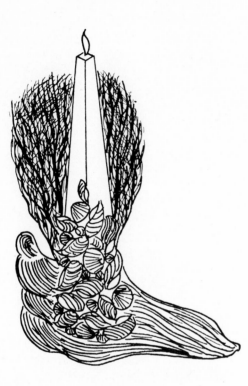

Figure 120

DOILIES AND DECOUPAGE

There are so many ways that doilies or decoupage can be affixed to candles. With a little artistic imagination you can dream up all sorts of designs and patterns to adorn your prize candles.

From Juanita Huston of Medina, Ohio: "With a tall round taper candle I attach gold lace-paper doilies, centered with big sequins. This stands on a base of five of these doilies arranged in a circle."

From Mary Pruden: "Dip lace and lace medallions into hot wax and quickly apply to the candle while still *wet*. White lace on deep-toned candles is very effective; on a deep blue it has a wedgewood look."

From Mrs. C. C. Dunkle of Pinehurst, Idaho: "I had a mold made at a tin shop which was four inches at the top and tapered to three inches at the bottom. I poured a red candle and removed the corners with a hot knife; also ran the knife around the edges. For trim, I applied gold lace, medallion and leaves. The medallion is centered with a plastic strawberry and star sets pinned on" (See Figure 121. Pictures 52 and 53 also show how decoupage may be used).

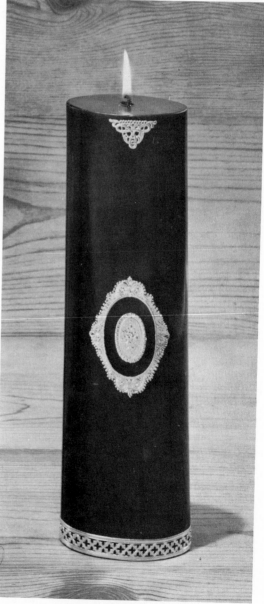

Picture 52

Picture 53

Figure 121

RIBBON AND LACE

Frankly, we didn't realize how adaptable ribbon and lace were for decorating candles until we heard from Bernice Killis of Vancouver, Washington. The following three creations by Miss Killis, featuring ribbon and lace, certainly reaffirmed our beliefs that with a little resourcefulness and imagination one can do just about anything with the right materials (See Picture 54). Bernice explains:

"On a round white hurricane I glue a few foil butterflies (purchased at a stationer's store). Then cover the shell with a netting, using any slow-drying glue. I then add silver rick-rack at the top and bottom and a fence of pearls around the top edge, secured with pins. This makes a very dainty candle—an especially nice gift for a new mother.

"On a three-inch square or pyramid candle I ran lacelon ribbon down all four sides, securing it with a slow-drying glue. While the glue was still wet, I sprinkled on some metallic stars. I then pinned on larger stars or other sequins.

"Cover a pink square hurricane with lacelon ribbon (purchased at most variety stores). Attach with any slow-drying glue. Use rick-rack or any silver braid and attach with glue and/or half-pins around the top and bottom. For an added touch, place pearls or sequins between the rows of rick-rack. Add grapes on all four sides with half-pins or glue pearls on the tips of each leaf. This makes a very attractive candle and can be used the year around."

CARD PICTURES

You'll discover a wealth of material for candle-decorating by rummaging through old Christmas cards. You'll find numerous colorful designs and pictures for a wide-candle surface; all you have to do is cut these out and hold them with glue or pins. They may be used alone or in conjunction with other decorations, such as sequins, glitter, decoupage and whipped wax.

Picture 54

Mrs. F. O. Ware discloses her method of combining pictures with medallions: "Recently I discovered that by cutting out the center part of a gold medallion and using the outer section as a frame, I can insert pictures of either people to whom I'm giving the candle or pictures in color of our Minnesota scenery. Either simply or in pairs, they are quite effective. I use the large square taper mold for this type of candle, and put the frame on the side about half way up. Use gold strips at the bottom and top of the candle as a finishing touch."

Whipped wax supplements snow-scene pictures particularly well by giving the illusion of three dimensions. Merely cut out and pin or glue the picture to the candle, prepare your whipped wax and apply it around the picture so that it will blend in with the over-all scene (See Picture 55).

Picture 55

If you are fortunate enough to find a card with a picture of a stained glass window, you can create a truly beautiful display. Adhere the picture of the window on to the candle and build up a frame of whipped wax around it, also covering the entire candle with a layer of whipped wax. This is particularly effective with a hurricane candle where the votive candle glows from within, thus giving the impression of a glowing church window on a snowy, wintry night (See Figure 122).

Figure 122

If you want to give those newly weds a present they'll greatly appreciate and cherish, make a white block candle, then cut out their wedding picture from the newspaper and pin it on the candle with corsage pins (See Figure 179).

You may either leave the candle as it is or decorate it further with whipped wax or sequins.

DRIED MATERIALS

Most of us enjoy "getting away from it all" by taking an occasional walk in the park or country. Next time you spend a few leisure hours this way look for such dried materials as cones, pods and plants to adorn your candles. For autumn candles, these items are "a natural" and cost nothing more than the time it takes to gather them.

Dried flowers may also be used, but must be prepared beforehand. Ruth Flanders of Portland, Oregon, writes: "The most interesting candles I've created have been decorated with dried flowers on a candle poured from a Pourette pyramid mold. The flowers must be selected and dried carefully before applying to the candle; must be small and flat. Pansies and baby breath are beautiful. The color of the candle must harmonize with the flower. Red candles decorated with pine cones and gold ribbon are also very popular."

Miss Flanders' enthusiasm for dried flowers and materials is also shared by numerous other candle hobbyists throughout the country. This is understandable for several reasons: natural decorations are particularly appealing, since you can't improve on nature; it's fun and relaxing gathering such items; and there's no cost involved unless you purchase the items from a floral shop as is sometimes necessary.

Through our correspondence we have received and assembled several ideas featuring dried materials.

Mrs. George Shepphird of San Gabriel, California, reveals her secrets for using dried materials: "I collect seed pods, acorns, burs and cones to create nosegays which I pin to the base of the candles. Sometimes I make wreaths of the natural materials to surround the candle and collect unusual

Figure 123

pieces of bark and driftwood to combine with lichens and cones as containers or foregrounds."

From Mrs. Jess Togdon of Anadarko, Oklahoma: "Some of our prettiest candles were decorated with glittered pine cone flowers. These were made by sawing the cones in thin pieces cross-wise; then glued and glittered the center and edges; wired them and pushed the wire into the candle. On a brown candle they were beautiful (See Figure 123).

Large "pine cone poinsettias" can also be created to decorate a plain candle. The "petals" are cut from large-size pine cones, painted red and sprinkled with red glitter. The petals are then forced into a small wad of gold sheet beeswax or a styrofoam ball painted gold. The completed "flowers" are then affixed directly to the candle or secured to sprigs of pine or any variety of greens available and situated about the candle base for an attractive arrangement (See Group Picture IV, Page 80d.)

From Mrs. Leona Harnden of Stillwater, Oklahoma: "I went to the country and cut stalks of wheat while they were still green. The grains will not shatter so badly when green. I dipped the wheat into hot wax and then placed it on the prepared candle. I rolled the candle in waxed paper and then in a terry cloth towel to press the wheat into the wax, or hold it against the candle till the wax could cool and hold it in place. If

needed, I painted it with additional wax. The wheat was later painted gold. Around the bottom of the candle I pressed a scalloped band of foil mesh, secured with a sequin pin. To keep the foil mesh from scratching a table top, I fastened a very thin circle of styrofoam to the bottom of the candle."

Mrs. Harnden uses dried foilage in much the same manner. "I applied whipped wax to a round candle and before it had completely cooled, I warmed it with my hair dryer over the area where I wanted to apply the foilage. I then placed the foilage on a piece of wax paper with a bath towel underneath and laid the warmed side of the candle on the foilage. I wrapped the candle with the towel and pressed the area where the foilage had been placed. I painted the foilage with a brush dipped in hot wax to fasten the edges down. Then the candle was dipped in the glaze" (See Picture 57).

From Mrs. Raymond DeBriar of Cathlamet, Washington: "I made a spray of small cones and arranged them on a round candle. To make the spray, start with a length of wire the length you want the spray and wire a small cone to the top. Next, take short lengths of wire and wire a cone to each short length; twist short lengths around the main wire, making them fill in solidly. When the spray is assembled, spray the cones and wire gold or any color. Use concealed sequin pins to secure the spray to the candle."

Picture 57

Miscellaneous Decorating Techniques

We have now covered some of the most common decorating techniques. Some not-so-common techniques are constantly being devised by creative individuals. Some of these have been passed along to us. Here they are:

From Mrs. E. C. Horne of Denver, Colorado: "A yellow three-inch round candle with a yellow, white and black real butterfly, and real preserved maidenhair fern glued on. The butterfly is sprayed with plastic (See Figure 125).

From Mrs. Leona Harnden: "On one candle surfaced with whipped wax I pinned laquered holly leaves" (See Figure 126).

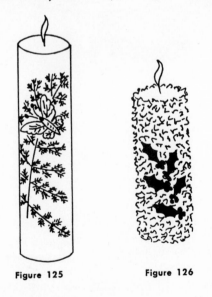

| Figure 125 | Figure 126 |

Juanita Huston of Medina, Ohio, contributes three ideas:

"The two- or three-inch round candle is effective for children's parties when several are grouped together; all one color or various colors to follow a color scheme. These are studded with small gumdrops that have been attached by inserting pins into the candle at random, then slipping gumdrops over the head of each pin. This is both decorative and edible (See Group Picture IV, Page 80d.)

"I made many of the five-pointed star taper candles using two sizes of nailheads and various colors. One of the most effective was a deep bright red star upon which I used the pearl nailheads alternating large and small; very impressive with soft greenery around the base. The white stars are lovely when decorated with gold star sequins.

"I made a five-pointed white star taper for our Eastern Star lodge. The five points were decorated in the colors of Eastern Star (green, red, blue, yellow and white) using alternating large and small nailheads."

From Orva Eberling of Colorado Springs, Colorado: "The things one can do with two- or three-inch round candles are almost endless. For example, take the two-inch round, use decorative scotch tape at intervals around the length of the candle. Take the three-inch round, wrap diagonally with a plain color tape, and use star sequins between the diagonal tape."

Mrs. Gale Williamson of Pemberville, Ohio, offers another idea: "Decorate with spray-on-snow over a colored candle to desired thickness and then add any other accessory for decoration."

Miss Vicki Willder of Honolulu, Hawaii, suggests a Stix-On Metallic Tape she located in a local store. This tape is ideal for sticking around the base of a cylindrical candle,

Picture 58

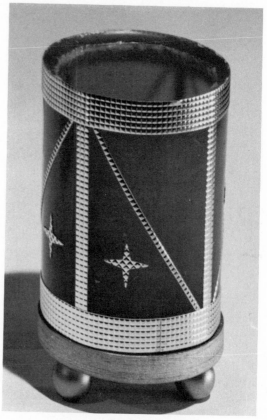

Picture 59

for it not only provides the finishing touch but hides any unevenness on the bottom edge of the candle. This type may also be cut in varying widths and applied on the candle in numerous shapes or designs (See Pictures 58 and, 59).

Gummed colored tape may also be applied in a similar fashion if so desired.

Speaking of gummed articles, Mary Pruden suggests using gummed Christmas seals or other "stickers" attached with rubber ce-

ment on candle. She adds: "Paint over them with a thin film of clear, hot wax to give a protective coating and to make certain they stick."

Even with these additional ideas, the list of decorating material is by no means exhausted—we've merely scratched the surface. Perhaps, however, these suggestions will start you thinking along daring lines and ultimately enable you to think up some of your own original techniques.

Mr. and Mrs. Leonard Olsen examined a candle formed in the star mold he held,
one of the candlemaking supplies produced by Pourette Mfg. Co.

PART IV

YEAR-AROUND DECORATING IDEAS

The Four Seasons

From the "how-to" portion of candle decorating we proceed to the "when-to" phase of the art.

A knowledge of inside trade secrets is not enough—equally important is the *how* and *when* of those secrets.

Winter Candles

Of the four seasons, none offer the candle hobbyist as much opportunity to create—as the winter season. Particularly during the Christmas holidays—when the spirit of friendship and goodwill prevail so strongly—does the soft, friendly glow of candlelight lend itself so appropriately. They add warmth and cheerfulness to a home (See Picture 60).

Picture 60—Winter candles created by Mrs. Arnold Johnson

CHRISTMAS CANDLES

Submitted by Sam Disney of Cincinnati, Ohio (See Figure 128). In a large square or round mold cut a shadow box about ½″ deep with a pointed instrument. Place a small figurine, such as an angel, inside. Frame the shadow box by cutting out the center from a large golden seal or medallion and pin it around the edge of the hole. Trim the base of the candle with a gold border strip.

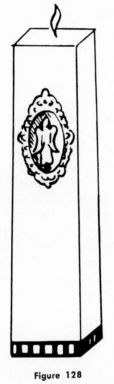

Figure 128

Large "snow"-covered tree (See Picture 61). Apply whipped wax to a large cone-shaped candle. Spray small pine cones or alder cones gold and insert around the surface of the whipped wax while the latter is still wet. Apply various sequins, if desired.

Noel Candle, submitted by Mrs. Stanley Huston (See Picture 62). On any large mold adhere gold, self-adhesive letters N-O-E-L down one side. Insert small gold nailheads to the side and back of the candle.

Picture 61

Toy train scene (See Picture 63). Pour a light blue or pink round hurricane candle. Apply a Meyercord Decal of a toy train or cut one from a Christmas card and affix it around the candle. Apply whipped wax around base and dabs of wax behind smoke-stack to resemble puffing smoke.

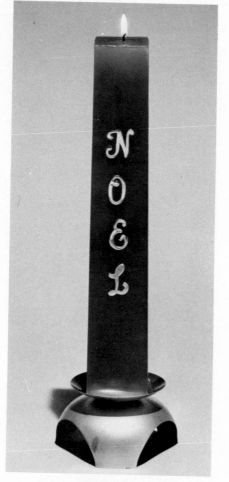

Submitted by Mrs. Stanley Huston. Make a three-inch square candle and attach Christmas designs from old cards or Rineglas transfers to each side. Apply whipped wax to cover areas not covered by the design and slightly over the raw edges of the design to conceal them. Add a few sprigs of pine or greenery around the base.

Decorated snowball (See Picture 64). Make a round candle from a round cereal bowl or round mold and apply whipped wax. Insert clusters of artificial holly leaves and berries into the whipped wax.

Submitted by Mrs. Ethel Black of Andover, Connecticut. On red three-inch round candle personalize it by writing such greeting as "Merry Christmas to John" directly on the candle. Write in a spiral pattern around the candle, or more formally, one word above the other. Write the name with a tube of Glitter Magic or Glue 'n Glitter, a glue premixed with glitter for spot application; or apply the cement first with a small brush, then dust with glitter. Scatter small clusters of real or artificial holly and berries near the names (See Group Picture III, Page 80c.)

Picture 63

Picture 64

Small snow-covered tree (See Picture 4). Apply whipped wax to a small cone-shaped candle formed from a cone-shaped dixie cup. Insert small colored sequins into the wax to resemble Christmas tree ornaments.

Submitted by Mrs. E. C. Horne of Denver, Colorado (See Figure 129). On a three-inch white candle adhere a cluster of gold-painted wax holly leaves and gold Christmas balls for berries. Dust the leaves with gold glitter for added sparkle.

Figure 129

Beeswax hurricane candle. Wrap and fit a red sheet of beeswax around a red hurricane candle. Place candle on a six-inch diameter base of styrofoam; apply whipped wax around the base and top edge of the candle. Insert small plastic reindeer into the "snow" around the base while still wet (See Group Picture II, Page 80b.)

Decorated hurricane candle (See Picture 66). Pour a clear white hurricane candle and apply whipped wax around the base. Insert into the whipped wax while still wet three clusters of silver leaves; assemble with pink and silver ornaments and spikes.

Decorated hurricane candle (See Picture 66). Wrap and fit a red sheet of beeswax around a red hurricane candle. Apply whipped wax around the base and along upper edge to conceal edges of beeswax. Insert small colored ornaments into the whipped wax.

Decorated hurricane candle (See Picture 66). Wrap and fit around a white hurricane candle any bright colored beeswax sheet. Pin a gold border strip around the base and top and a medallion in the center of each side.

Picture 66

Submitted by Mrs. G. A. Culpepper (See Figure 131). Insert a red, tall, round tapered candle in a styrofoam base. Make three large red wax bells from a glass goblet, lining the rims with gold glitter. Attach the bells to the candle with red and gold metallic ribbon. Cover styrofoam with flocked pine cones.

Submitted by Mary Pruden (See Figure 132). Pour about ¼″ of green or red wax into a flat pan and let it set up until it can be handled without sticking to your fingers. Cut into 3″ strips; roll on a warm surface with the palms of your hands into a long rope about ½″ thick. If it begins to stiffen before you finish, place it near a warm radiator or oven to make it pliable again. If you work quickly, just the heat of your hands will be enough. Quickly spiral the "rope" around a white candle from top to bottom. A little hot wax can be dribbled on to seal it to the candle.

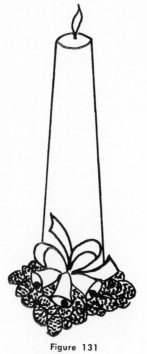

Figure 131

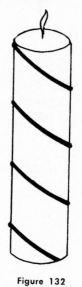

Figure 132

Angel decorated candle. Pour a deep blue square or diamond shaped candle. Cut four 2″ lengths of wire from a coat hanger. Heat the wire lengths on your stove burner (holding them with pliers) and press into the sides of the candle. Insert them in pairs, about an inch apart, at two different levels and on adjoining sides of the candle. When inserting the wire lengths, lay the candle on its side and hold each length steady, pressing it into the wax until it cools enough to permit the wax to cool around it. Each length will then remain rigidly in place. Affix a wad of cotton around the wire lengths, now extending from the candle, and place additional cotton loosely around the base. Upon the two small "clouds" set two angels (See Group Picture II, Page 80b.)

Chimney candle (See Picture 67). Pour a clear white hurricane candle. With a 1″ or 2″ brush, "paint" the outside of the candle with a coat of deep red wax, using vertical strokes. The wax should be at least 190°; two coats are usually required for adequate covering, letting the first coat set completely before applying the second. With a ruler and ice pick, scribe lines on the red coating to use as a guide when carving later with a V-groover or linoleum carver. Follow the lines previously made with a V-groover, gouging through the red "bricks" down to the white "mortar." Set on a styrofoam base and apply whipped wax around top of "chimney" and at the base.

Picture 67

with rays of small gold rick-rack, extending down the creche. Add a band of brown whipped wax around the bottom edge for a finishing effect.

Submitted by Mrs. Leslie Townsend of St. Louis, Missouri (See Figure 134). Pour a red cone-shaped candle. Cut a Santa face from a Christmas card, dip it in hot white wax and press it near the base of the candle. Apply whipped wax whiskers and white hair. Pin a white tassel by the wick. Place candle on a large round base with four wooden ball feet glued on.

Figure 134

Submitted by Mrs. Stanley Huston (See Figure 133). Pour a soft-brown, large-cone candle. Hollow out an area near the bottom and insert a small plastic nativity scene. Near the top secure a crystal or gold star

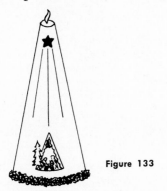

Figure 133

Santa Claus head candle (See Picture 68). Pour bright red wax into a cone mold until it is about a third full and let set for approximately two hours. Fill the remaining two-thirds of the mold with pink wax. Apply eyes, nose and mouth out of one or a combination of the following: Painted on with wax, crayon or paint; cut out of thin layers of wax; cut from beeswax sheets; cut out of colored paper, felt, etc. Apply whipped wax to resemble whiskers, moustache, eyebrows and trim on the cap.

Picture 68

wick extending down from bottom of top candle into the hole and press the two forms together. Let stand until the wax adhering the two forms has completely hardened. Green or red glitter may be sprinkled on the finished candle if a more vivid display is desired. Pin pine branch into place and tie a ribbon around center of candle to conceal the joint. Attach bells with a bow (See Group Picture I, Page 80a.)

The Star Sprinklers. It pays to keep a watchful eye on your old Christmas cards for they often provide clever ideas for candle decorating (See Group Picture III, Page 80c.) The little angels were cut from a card and pinned onto a white hexagon candle with half-pins. Small gold star sequins were affixed at random and gold glitter sprinkled on (with the help of glitter cement) to denote "star dust."

Submitted by Leslie Townsend (See Figure 135). Here again Christmas cards were put to use. Cut out church windows from cards and adhere to sides of a white hurricane candle with hot wax. Cover the remaining part of the candle surrounding the windows with whipped wax. Place the candle on a Pourette square hurricane base tinted with gold glitter.

Submitted by Mrs. Robert Kamrath of Wilson, Texas. Make two wax forms from a small mold, such as a dixie cup or small drinking glass, making one green and the other red; scent and insert wick into only one of the forms. If made from a dixie cup, it may be necessary to buff the wax surface lightly to acquire a sheen. Make a small hole in the small end of the base form and apply a small, flat ring of wax-weld around the hole. Fill the hole with liquid wax, lower

Figure 135

Angel hurricane candle (See Picture 69 and Group Picture I, Page 80a.) Pour a red or light blue square hurricane candle. Form four white angels from a Pourette angel mold and adhere to sides of hurricane with wax weld. Four green trees may also be used as alternates. Set on a square styrofoam base and apply whipped wax to both the base and top edge of candle.

Picture 69

A wax angel submitted by Leslie Townsend (See Figure 136). Pour pale pink, ice blue or white wax in a pilsner glass and ping-pong ball halves. Join the two halves formed from the ping-pong balls and attach to the top of the "body" formed from the pilsner glass. Dip the attached head into wax until it is firmly attached. Apply sequins for the eyes and mouth and whipped wax sprinkled with copper glitter for the hair. Place the body on a cardboard circle and apply a ruffle of whipped wax around the bottom of the form. Cut out and pin on aluminum foil wings and halo.

Figure 136

Submitted by Mrs. Frank Rittmueller of Frankenmuth, Michigan (See Figure 137). Spray a six-pointed star candle silver. Affix small round blue Christmas tree ornaments in each depression.

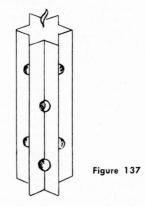

Figure 137

Christmas-tree hurricane candle (See Picture 70). Pour a green square hurricane candle. Cut a length of coat hanger and shape it to resemble the outline of a Christmas tree (See Figure 138). Place the "branding iron" face down on your stove burner until well heated. Lay the hurricane shell on its side, insert a piece of paper inside to catch any drippings, and press the "iron" into the side

Picture 70

Figure 138

until it melts through the wax. If the iron isn't hot enough or the hurricane walls are exceptionally thick, the iron may not go through the wax on the first try. Don't force it! Withdraw the iron, remove excess wax and reheat for a second try. Don't panic when you see molten wax welling out over the smooth wax surface as you press in the iron. This can't be avoided but can be concealed later with decorations such as sequins, glitter, etc. Repeat the process for each side. The outlined trees may be decorated with sequins, whipped wax, paint or glitter. The wax outside the tree may also be decorated with glitter or diamond dust.

Submitted by Mrs. W. H. Dumeyer of Salisbury, Maryland (See Figure 139). Make a blue three-inch square or pyramid candle. Attach a white wax angel made from a Pourette plastic mold near the base of the candle. Make a halo over her head with gold or silver glitter, depending upon the color of the candle.

Figure 139

Chimney candle (See Picture 71). Pour a red three-inch square candle. Apply Rineglas gold strips cut from gold Rineglas sheets to resemble mortar in a brick chimney. Secure "chimney" to a styrofoam base and apply whipped wax around base and top to resemble snow.

Picture 71

Submitted by Leslie Townsend (See Figure 140). Place a red or green six-pointed star candle on a six-pointed star styrofoam base. Cover the styrofoam with whipped wax and insert tiny pine cones and artificial berries.

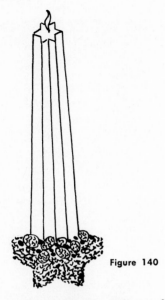

Figure 140

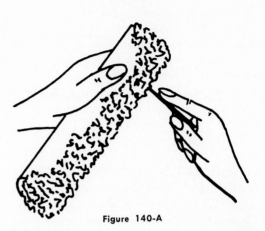

Figure 140-A

Submitted by Mrs. Charles Glynn of Patterson, California (See Figure 141). Impress small stars with a cookie cutter on a large red block candle. Fill in the stars with silver glitter and "connect" them with a swish of glitter. Cut three stars from thin sheets of wax and cover with silver glitter. Place the candle on a styrofoam base, apply whipped wax to the styrofoam and insert the stars upright into the whipped wax while still soft.

Yule log. Make a brown "log" from a three-inch round mold; do not insert wick. Score the log along sides with a wire brush or hand saw to give the illusion of rough bark. Apply whipped wax along one side to resemble snow and drill or poke with a heated ice pick three wick holes through the "snow" and insert wick (See Figure 140-A, also Group Picture I, Page 80a.)

Submitted by Mrs. Charles Glynn (See Figure 142). Pour a pale green or blue three-

Figure 141

Figure 142

inch candle. Cut out from an old Christmas card an old-fashioned street lantern and pin-prick the outline on to the side of the candle. Paint along the pin-pricks with a melted crayon. Apply whipped wax around top of candle, along top of lantern and around the candle base. Sprinkle on a glitter design as a background to the lantern, or as an alternate background you may apply real or artificial sprigs of pine.

Christmas bell candle (See Picture 28). On any large block candle either tie or pin wax bells to the center. The wax bells are formed from drinking glasses as previously described.

Frosted candle, submitted by Mrs. Blake Kinnear of Seldovia, Alaska (See Figure 143). Brush melted uncolored wax with a ½″ or 1″ brush on to surface of any large block candle. If brushed on briskly, it gives the candle the appearance of a heavy frost.

Picture 73

Figure 143

Nativity scene candle (See Picture 73). Pour a light-blue triangular or square candle. Hold small nativity scene against side of candle while applying whipped wax around it. When wax sets, the scene will be held firmly in place.

Submitted by Mrs. Charles Russell (See Figure 144). Insert a red six-pointed star candle into a round styrofoam base. Affix Christmas ornaments, lacquered leaves, and ornamental spikes between the points. Coat styrofoam base with paint or glitter.

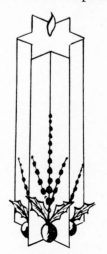

Figure 144

Christmas-tree hurricane candle (See Picture 74). Pour a tall, pale-blue, round hurricane candle. Pin on a cedar sprig to resemble a Christmas tree, decorating the tree with sequins, bells, etc. Apply whipped wax around the base and top of candle for finishing touch.

Submitted by Jay Bottger (See Figure 146). Sprinkle gold glitter on a large, round, red candle. Pin on holly leaves with Pourette holly-berry pins. Affix a gold border strip around the base.

Figure 146

Picture 74

Submitted by Jay Bottger of Spokane, Washington (See Figure 145). Apply whipped wax along a spiraling line around a red or green cone-shaped candle. Insert small birthday candles every few inches along the whipped-wax "ledge."

Submitted by Mrs. R. Kamrath of Wilson, Texas (See Picture 75). Pin gold ric-rac on a dark-green, cone-shaped candle in a spiral pattern. Pin gold snowflakes or leaf sequins between the spiraling ric-rac. Affix the candle to a four-inch diameter, two-inch thick wooden base painted gold.

Submitted by Mrs. R. Kamrath (See Figure 147). Pour three or four candles from a gelatin mold. Sprinkle each candle with silver glitter and place on a 12″ piece of 2x4 covered with foil. The foil may also be dusted with silver glitter. Use as a low table centerpiece and surround with spruce greenery and small ornaments.

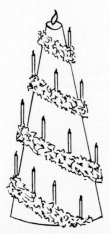

Figure 145

Figure 147

Picture 75

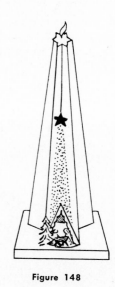

Figure 148

Submitted by Mrs. Charles Glynn (See Figure 149). Paint holly and berries on a three-inch square candle with colored wax or wax paint. Paint leaves dark green; berries, silver; with silver glitter in center of berries. Paint remainder of candle around designs with swishes of silver paint, using uneven strokes. Insert candle in a styrofoam base; cover base with whipped wax; insert artificial holly leaves and berries; paint whipped wax silver and dust with silver glitter.

Another submitted by Mrs. R. Kamrath (See Figure 148). Pour a blue six-pointed star candle and trace around its base on a piece of styrofoam. Dig out the interior section of the outlined star, attach a little floral clay or wax weld and insert the candle. Apply whipped wax on the styrofoam and press a nativity scene into the wax between two points of the candle. Affix a large silver star sequin above the nativity scene and sprinkle glitter between the star and scene.

Figure 149

Christmas candy tree. Submitted by Mrs. H. Teinert of Slaton, Texas (See Picture 76). Coat a green cone-shaped candle with white whipped wax. While wax is still soft insert small candies and sprinkle with gold glitter.

Picture 76

Pine cone poinsettia candle. If you have some large pine cones on hand, you're in luck as far as this candle is concerned. Clip off the larger "petals" from the base of the cone, paint each petal red and sprinkle on red glitter. When the petals have dried insert seven into a small wad of gold sheet beeswax to resemble a poinsettia. Brush cooled liquid wax on to a white candle, sprinkling the surface with diamond dust as you apply the wax so that the glitter will adhere to the candle surface. Position the "poinsettia blossoms" on to the candle and secure them in place by pressing a pin through the gold beeswax center into the side of the candle. A few loose "flowers" may be placed at the candle base, if desired (See Group Picture IV, Page 80d.)

Madonna candle. Submitted by Mrs. Helen Medin. Pour a lavender star candle and secure it to a round piece of plywood (8″ diameter) that has been sprayed gold. The candle may be secured with a heavy floral clay, such as "Cling" or wax weld. Spray gold a Madonna figure, artificial poinsettias and forget-me-nots; position the Madonna at the front and arrange the gold artificial flowers about the base, adhering them with the same floral clay used to secure the candle firmly. A felt covering glued to the underside of the plywood base eliminates the danger of marring your table top (See Group Picture IV, Page 80d.)

NEW YEARS CANDLES

Midnight candle. Submitted by Mrs. Stanley Huston (See Picture 77). Pour a black oval candle. Design a symmetrical oval pattern of the hour spots of a clock on a paper. Place the pattern on your candle and pinprick the hour spots on to the candle surface. Insert nailheads or upholstery tacks into the 12 hour spots. Cut out and attach with a large nailhead two clock hands pointing to the midnight hour. The hands may be made from tag board painted gold; gold border strips of Rineglas transfers. Confetti and taped curls may be arranged around base.

Champagne candle (See Picture 78). Pour a black three-inch round candle. Paint with silver paint a tilted champagne glass, half filled, with bubbles rising from the bottom of the glass. Apply silver Stix-On-Metallic-Tape around base of candle and affix cupped sequins or small cut-out sections from the tape to resemble the effervescence rising from the glass.

Picture 77

Picture 78

VALENTINE CANDLES

Submitted by Mrs. Harry A. Anderson of South Bend, Indiana (See Figure 150). Pour a white, large block candle, brush it with white wax, and sprinkle with diamond dust. Pour red wax into a cookie sheet and cut out red hearts before wax completely cools. Before "frosting" on candle has cooled, press hearts on to surface of candle. If hearts are to be applied to a round candle, warm them in warm water just prior to application, thus making them pliable enough to fit the contour of the candle.

Figure 151

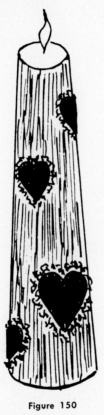

Figure 150

Submitted by Mrs. R. V. Cooper of Cedar Falls, Iowa (See Figure 151). Pour red or white, large block candle. Shape red or white hearts from chenille pipe cleaners and attach to candle with glue or Scotch tape. Insert candle on a styrofoam base covered with red or white crepe paper and a ribbon of the opposite color. Affix a nylon lace ruffle at the candle base for the finishing touch.

Submitted by Mrs. D. E. Bourrie of Plainfield, Illinois (See Figure 152). Pour a white octangular taper candle and insert into a six-inch round styrofoam base. To decorate the base, take a piece of red net approximately 9" x 72", fold it in half and gather it on a piece of spool wire. Fit this to the candle with the open end of the net in front; twist the wire ends together and hide the end. Join net together with a white artificial rose, using the wire stem to bind the two sides. Secure four other white roses to the netting equally spaced around the candle, securely binding the wire stems to the underside. Tie a 14" length of ⅝" red satin ribbon bow around last four roses. Tie a 30" length of ⅝" red satin around the base of the candle; make a bow and leave the ends long so they will trail along each side of the rose in the front-center. Cut out three hearts from wax or paper and affix to candle, using double-faced Scotch tape,

Figure 152

Picture 79

Cut out of heavy red paper two cupids and attach one on each side of a wire covered with white crepe paper. Stick this cupid through the net and into the styrofoam base at either side of the candle.

Beeswax heart candle (See Picture 79). Pour a tall, white, round taper candle. Cut out four varying sizes of hearts from a red sheet of beeswax, using a paper pattern as a guide. Press the hearts on to the candle, arranging them so that the smaller hearts are located nearer the top of the candle. A beeswax arrow may be pressed on one or two of the hearts to denote cupid's arrow.

Submitted by Mrs. George R. Shepphird of San Gabriel, California (See Picture 80). Make a red shell of wax from a heart-shaped cake tin as you would make a hurricane candle. If you need reviewing on the procedure, fill heart-shaped tin with red melted wax; allow to set for thirty minutes; cut ⅜"

from around the edge; lift out congealed surface and pour out the remaining liquid wax. When the "shell" has completely hardened, remove from mold, spray with glitter cement, and sprinkle gold glitter around the side. Place decorated shell on a paper lace doily, and position a tall red candle in the center; fill shell with water and surround center candle with floating gardenias.

Heart-shaped candle (See Figure 153). Again using a heart-shaped cake tin, pour two red hearts; gouge a groove down center of one heart and lay wick along groove. With wick in the groove "cement" the two hearts together with whipped wax applied around edge. Leave bottom inch of point bare for insertion into styrofoam base. Gouge out 1½″ hole in center of a six-inch round styrofoam block and insert tip of heart into hole. Apply whipped wax to base, piling it around tip of heart to assure stableness. Sequins may be applied to the whipped wax for added decoration.

Picture 80   **Figure 153**

MISCELLANEOUS WINTER CANDLES

Snowflake candle using doilies (See Picture 81). Pour a black or blue large square or round candle. Cut out small sections of a white doily which resemble snowflakes, dip in clear melted wax and press them immediately on the candle surface. They may be fixed on to the candle at random or in a spiraling snowfall pattern down around the candle with the larger "flakes" near the base.

Snowflake candle using Rineglas transfers (See Picture 82). Pour a black large square or round candle. Apply snowflakes from a Rineglas transfer. Pin small silver cupped sequins within the snowflake for added sparkle. Brush on icicles around the top of the candle with clear white wax and a very small brush for added effect. "Snow" may also be brushed on around the base.

Picture 81

Picture 82

Snowflake candle using glitter (See Figure 154 and Group Picture III, Page 80c.) Pour a pale-green or blue, large round or square candle. Design some simple but colorful snowflake patterns on paper using three or four colors. Lay the paper designs on the candle and pin-prick through the outline onto the candle surface. Follow the pin-pricks with glitter cement, using a small brush and sprinkle on the desired colored glitter. A tube of either Glitter Magic or Glue 'n Glitter may also be used. Allow each separate color to dry completely between applications to prevent the colors from overlapping or mixing.

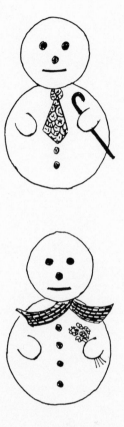

Figure 155

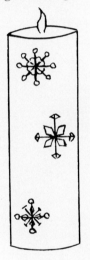

Figure 154

Snowman candle. Submitted by Leslie Townsend (See Figure 155). With two different sized round bowls or molds, pour two snowballs and join together creating the head and body of a snowman. Apply appropriate sequins for eyes, nose, mouth and buttons. Make a pair denoting a man and wife, applying accessories to dress them up . . . such as a ribbon tie and a pipe-cleaner cane for the man and a wool scarf of yarn and a little corsage of flowers for the woman.

Snow scene candle (See Group Picture IV, Page 80d.) Set a 9″ round aqua candle into a 1″-thick styrofoam base which is approximately 6″ by 12″. You may have to join two 6″ square pieces together to acquire such a broad base. Coat the entire styrofoam base with a spray artificial snow — secure the candle on one side and insert sprigs of evergreens such as pine, cedar, fir, etc., in the foreground and on each side of the candle. Lightly spray the sprigs and candle with the "snow"— place two or three snow birds on the boughs and your winter display is complete.

Spring and Summer Candles

ST. PATRICK'S DAY CANDLES

Submitted by Mrs. Clyde Jordan of Hazelwood, North Carolina (See Figure 156). Pour a white square hurricane candle. Cut out shamrocks, using either your own pattern or a cookie cutter, from a thin layer of green wax poured on to a cookie sheet. Attach a shamrock on each side of the candle with wax weld. A sequin design may be pinned on to each shamrock for added effect. Place candle on a six-inch square styrofoam base and apply whipped wax around candle base and along upper edge.

Figure 156

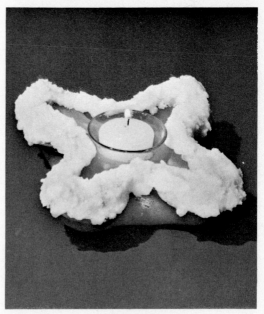

Figure 157

Top hat with shamrock (See Figure 157). Pour a four-inch black round candle and a layer of black wax in a greased pie tin. Wrap green ribbon around the "hat," securing it with half pins. Set the black candle on the "hat brim" of black wax and attach a shamrock made of either green tag board or wax to the front of the hat.

Clover-leaf candle (See Picture 83). Pour a ¼" layer of green wax into an 8" square pie tin. When the wax has set enough to maintain its shape and yet be pliable enough to bend—remove from the pan. From this layer of green wax mold a clover-shape form by pressing in the four sides of the wax and shape all edges upwards to form a shell. Refill center of formed leaf with green molten wax, insert wick and your St. Patrick's Day candle is ready to display as a centerpiece. An alternate method of furnishing a wick would be to place a votive glass in the center of the leaf before refilling with wax. This method would assure longer life of the candle for the votive candle placed in the glass is replaceable.

Picture 83

EASTER CANDLES

Wax Easter eggs. Submitted by Mary Pruden. Chip a ¼″ hole in the large end of an egg, punch a hole in the small end with a needle and shake the egg out into a bowl (for scrambled eggs, a cake or omelet). Rinse the inside of the shell with warm water and set aside to dry. These cleaned shells can be kept in egg boxes in a cool place so you will always have some on hand. Very carefully enlarge the needle hole to just fit the small metal core wicking. Thread the wick through, leaving about ¼″ outside the small hole (this is the top of the candle). Fold this tail of wick against the shell and tape to seal and prevent wax leakage. A corsage pin or long needle stuck through the other end of the wick will help keep it centered at the larger hole (See Figure 158-A). Stand the eggs, bottom side up, in an egg box and fill with the leftover wax in any color from your day's candlemaking. If the wax is cooled a bit before pouring, one refill should be enough. Set the box of eggs in the refrigerator to harden, then crack and peel off the shell. Pare a bit off the bottom or rub it on a hot pan to make it flat enough to stand well. Decorate with "jewels," sequins, pearls, glitter, decals, waxed flowers, sea shells or whipped wax. By dipping—they can be given a "shell" of a different color. Make them as gay as possible (See Figure 158-B).

Comment on Egg Candles: This is a good way to use up even the tiniest bits of colors. The shells may be filled with many different layers of colors. Just be sure the first layer has hardened before adding more, and the new wax must not be too hot. When hardened and the shells removed, you have a gaily striped egg. If the shells are tilted to one side until the last filling, the stripes will be on the diagonal.

Submitted by G. A. Culpepper (See Figure 159). Decorate blown eggs with sequins, glitter, braid, etc. Cut a hole at the base of each egg with a manicure scissors large enough in which a Christmas-tree light may be inserted. Position any large block candle on a 6″ square styrofoam base and affix the "connected eggs" about the base. Cover excess cord with whipped wax or Easter cellophane hay.

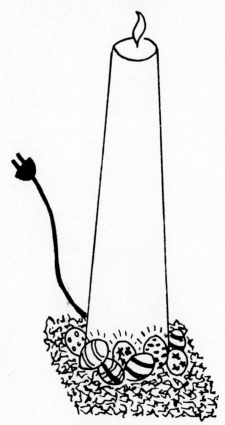

Figure 158-A   **Figure 158-B**

Figure 159

Cross candle (See Figure 160). With a two-inch square mold pour a 7″ and a 9″ wax form of white wax. Position the two forms to resemble the crosspiece and base of a cross, using the 7″ form as the base. Completely cover the forms with whipped wax, thus "cementing" them together. In the center of the crosspiece place a votive glass and apply whipped wax completely around it till it is well concealed and firmly attached to the crosspiece. Place the cross in a gouged-out hole in a six-inch square styrofoam block and cover with whipped wax. Place a votive candle in the glass and burn until it needs replacing.

Egg-shaped candle (See Figure 161). Procure two round bowls, one a little larger than the other. Fill both bowls with pink wax and remove when cooled. Apply a ½″ layer of whipped wax to flat surface of larger form and, while still wet, press smaller form on to it, flat side down. Apply band of whipped wax around center of "egg" to improve appearance and "cement" the two halves together, thus providing an egg-shaped form. Insert wick into top of egg with heated ice pick. Decorate remaining portion of egg with sequins, ric-rac, glitter, etc. Position egg on a white wax base formed from the pie tin.

Figure 160

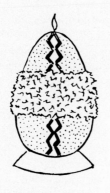

Figure 161

Easter rabbit (See Figure 162). Submitted by Mrs. Virginia Cummings of Schenectady, New York. Procure a round bowl and a smaller round cup. Pour a wax form from the bowl and two forms from the smaller mold "cementing" these two together with melted wax or wax weld to form the rabbit's head. Saw off a portion of the rounded part of the large form to provide a flat surface upon which to attach the "head." Shape the rabbit over the wax base form with whipped wax. Colored coconut may be sprinkled on to give a furry look. Ears can be cut from thin pink plastic foam and bent at a rakish angle. Whiskers are glittered pieces of wire; eyes are sequins and a ribbon tied around the neck completes the picture.

Wax Easter eggs may be easily created by using the balloon and water technique previously described. Merely fill a small round balloon with cold water, dip in wax repeatedly till desired thickness has been attained, remove balloon and decorate.

Submitted by Mrs. Bruce Sable of Washington, Michigan (See Figure 163). Pour a lavender, square, hurricane candle. Affix a pale yellow bunny or chicks to the sides. These may be flat appliques cut from wax or paper, or they may be three-dimensional, store-boughten figures.

Figure 163

Figure 162

Figure 164

Submitted by Mrs. Stanley Huston (See Figure 164). Pour a pastel, round tapered candle, approximately 10″ tall and place in a 16-oz. brandy snifter. The candle should extend above the top of the snifter an inch or so. Surround the candle within the snifter with large artificial flowers. The color harmonies with this display are tremendous and any decor color can be "picked up."

Submitted by Mrs. Clyde Jordan (See Figure 165). Pour a blue or lavender candle in a square, pyramid or triangular mold. With a small plastic "praying hands" mold and small cross mold pour white forms and affix to candle with wax weld.

Figure 166

Figure 165

Submitted by Mrs. C. C. Dunkle of Pinehurst, Idaho (See Figure 167). Pour a green or blue candle in a round bowl or half rubber ball. Pin on gold ric-rac around top edge with a green plastic fern and yellow wax rosebud attached to opposite sides. Cut wheels from layer of wax or small, round pieces of styrofoam dipped in wax. Attach store-boughten chicken to candle with yellow chenille "harness." You may make your own chicken out of styrofoam, connecting body and head with a pipe cleaner, spraying with yellow paint and affixing the bill, tail, legs and feet of yellow chenille.

Submitted by Mrs. R. C. Ebeling (See Figure 166). Form a candle from an egg-shaped canned ham can—inserting the wick after removal from the mold using the heated ice pick method. Glue Easter card picture such as an Easter lily, bunny or chick on one side. Shape the "egg" with the help of whipped wax.

Figure 167

MISCELLANEOUS SPRING CANDLES

Submitted by Mrs. Robert Cooper of
Cedar Falls, Iowa (See Figure 168). Pour
a pale-pink block candle. Affix a plastic
pink sweetpea stalk down one side and attach a pink fuzzy bird.

Figure 168

Pastel speckled candle. Using any block
candle mold, apply bits of pastel-colored
buds into your candle wall as explained previously on the section covering interior
decorated candles (See Group Picture III,
Page 80c.)

FOURTH OF JULY CANDLES

Red, white and blue layered candle. Use either a two- or three-inch round mold, and red, white and blue wax. Pour a layered candle as previously described (See Group Picture IV, Page 80d.)

Red, white and blue chunk candle. Using either a large round or square candle mold, apply red, white and blue wax chunks as described previously in the section on "Chunk Candles."

Fireworks candle (See Figure 169). Pour a black or blue large round candle. Apply sequins and glitter to resemble a fireworks display.

Figure 169

Picture 84

Spiraled glitter striped candle (See Picture 84). Pour a white, large, round candle. Lay out straight in multiples of three (3, 6, 9, 12, etc.) strips of masking tape approximately two feet in length, connecting them on each end with a strip of tape (See Figure 170-A). Beginning at the top of the candle, lay the masking tape at an angle, spiraling it down around the candle until it reaches the bottom (See Figure 170-B). Try to arrange the strips so that the entire candle is covered. Peel off every third strip, coat the exposed portion of wax with glitter cement and sprinkle on red glitter, let dry for approximately 24 hours (See Figure 170-C). Peel off the next strip and follow the same procedure except sprinkle this stripe with either silver glitter or diamond dust. For the third and last stripe use blue glitter. When completed you should have a glistening red, white and blue candle. Wider stripes may be acquired by peeling off two adjoining strips of tape at a time.

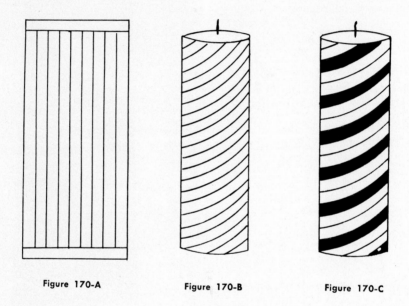

Figure 170-A   Figure 170-B   Figure 170-C

Fall Candles

HALLOWEEN

Solid pumpkin. Submitted by Mrs. Leona Harnden (See Picture 85). Acquire two jello molds or "Desert Rose" pattern teacups made by Franciscan Pottery. Pour two orange-colored forms and join them together to form a pumpkin. Carving may be necessary to provide authenticity, after which a dip in orange wax will smooth off the rough spots. An artificial leaf or two of green wax or other material near the top adds realism . . . for a pumpkin on the vine. If eyes, nose and mouth are desired, use either black wax paint, black glitter or sequins.

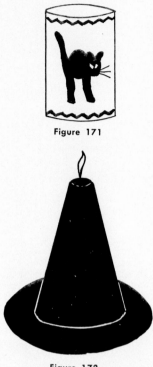

Figure 171

Figure 172

Submitted by Bernice Kellis (See Figure 171). Pour an orange round hurricane candle. Trim top and bottom edge with black ric-rac. Attach black cats (purchased at party shops) around center with black pins. Dust remainder of candle with gold glitter if desired.

Picture 85

Witch hat. Submitted by Mrs. Calvin Jones of Houston, Texas (See Figure 172). Pour a black cone shaped candle and set it on a ¼″ thick black base formed from pouring black wax into a pie tin.

Submitted by Lawrence Rowland of Wichita, Kansas (See Figure 173). Pour an orange round hurricane candle. Drill openings for eyes, nose and mouth through one side of the shell and complete pumpkin face by carving out the details. Paint inside surface of carved-out features with black paint and set on a hurricane base.

poured out, press a round cookie cutter into the center base. When wax has cooled and has been removed from the mold, snap out the round disc formed from the cookie cutter. Join the two halves by melting the joining edges a little first against a heated pie tin and pressing the two halves together. Figure 24 shows another step which may be taken to assure a good bond between the two halves. Merely swirl the seam through a little liquid wax in a pie tin. Paint on a pumpkin face with black paint or black glitter. Place a votive glass and candle in the center to provide a soft glow of light from within.

Figure 173

Picture 86

Spook candles. Submitted by Rose Kowalczyk of Brookfield, Illinois (See Picture 86). Pour white wax into four soft plastic juice glasses, let cool until the glasses feel slightly warm (about 20 minutes), then set in hot water for about a minute. Withdraw from glasses and squeeze top fourth of each form into a head shape and mold body by hand to resemble spooks. Insert wick with the ice pick method. Paint face with a small brush and melted black crayon. Some of the spooks may hold a little Jack-o-lantern (just a little orange ball of wax with a face painted on).

Hollow pumpkin (See Picture 87). Form two orange hurricane shells from a cereal bowl or similar shaped mold. On one of the halves, just after the center wax has been

Witch-on-a-broomstick candle (See Figure 174). Pour an orange round hurricane candle. Make a witch on a broomstick stencil by drawing and cutting out the figure from a large piece of paper. Pin the paper temporarily onto the side of the candle, so that the witch is positioned in the center. Paint the witch with black paint, using either a spray paint can or a small brush.

Figure 174

Hollow pumpkin (See Picture 87). Form two orange hurricane shells from a cereal bowl or similar shaped mold. On one of the halves, just after the center wax has been poured out, press a round cookie cutter into the center base. When wax has cooled and has been removed from the mold, snap out the round disc formed from the cookie cutter. Join the two halves by melting the joining edges a little first against a heated pie tin and pressing the two halves together. Figure 24 shows another step which may be taken to assure a good bond between the two halves. Merely swirl the seam through a little liquid wax in a pie tin. Paint on a pumpkin face with black paint or black glitter. Place a votive glass and candle in the center to provide a soft glow of light from within.

Little girl pumpkin. Submitted by Mrs. Corinne Cook of Seattle, Washington (See Picture 88). Form a hollow pumpkin—using the method previously described. Apply brown whipped wax to denote hair and insert a short green candle stub into the whipped wax on the removable lid at the top to provide a "stem" for the pumpkin. Cut and curl thin strips of black wax—insert them through the eyes adhering them on the interior with floral clay or wax weld. Once the pumpkin is formed, you are ready to create a base upon which to set it. The base shown in the picture consists of "plaster-of-paris" spread over an irregular cardboard base. While the plaster is soft press the pumpkin into the desired position—let the plaster set and then pour a coating of brown wax over the entire base. Cut and shape the "vine leaves" from a thin layer of green wax and position them around the pumpkin with either floral clay or wax weld. This Halloween creation is time consuming, but well worth the effort because of its quaintness and the fact that it may be re-used each Halloween thereafter.

Picture 87

Picture 88

THANKSGIVING, MISCELLANEOUS
FALL CANDLES

Submitted by Mrs. G. A. Culpepper (See Figure 175). Pour an autumn-colored large round or round tapered candle. Wire into a long garland small imitation fruits, shellacked nuts, holly and mistletoe berries. Spiral this garland around the candle and set candle in a white compote. Fill the compote with slightly larger fruits and nuts.

Submitted by Mrs. G. W. Beckwith of South Bend, Indiana (See Picture 89). Pour a rust colored hurricane candle. Apply whipped wax around the base and up corners of the candle. Embed artificial fruit, nuts and leaves of your choice into the whipped wax while it is still soft with the result resembling a Della Robbia effect.

Picture 89

Ear of corn candle. Submitted by Mrs. Clyde Jordan (See Figure 176). Pour two yellow halves of corn in a kitchen corn stick mold and "cement" together with wick inserted as previously described. Pour a thin layer of green wax onto a cookie sheet and when partially "set" cut out corn husks and shape around the "ear of corn." Place candle on a large spike candle holder to provide sturdiness.

Corn candle (See Figure 177). Pour a pale green 3″ square candle and four yellow halves of corn from a kitchen corn stick mold. Attach the halves of corn to the four sides of the candle with wax weld or melted wax. Cut and form by hand green corn husks from a thin layer of wax and press one leaf to each ear of corn.

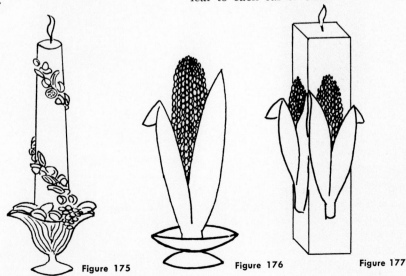

Figure 175　　　　**Figure 176**　　　　**Figure 177**

Picture 90

Picture 91

Conventional autumn candle (See Picture 90). Pour a rust-colored tall round taper candle. Pin cattails, wheat stalks and autumn leaves (artificial or real one dipped in wax) onto one side of the candle. Pin a gold border strip around the base.

Contemporary autumn candle (See Picture 91). Pour a black tall round taper candle. Spray sea oats and small cattails silver and pin onto side of candle. Pin a silver border strip around the base.

Picture 92

Submitted by Mrs. A. C. Graef of Canton, Ohio (See Picture 92, also Group Picture III, Page 80c. Pour a pale yellow or rust 3″ round candle. Form a darker rust cornucopia from a layer of wax or beeswax . . . or you may purchase a small woven reed cornucopia usually available just prior to Thanksgiving. Assemble artificial fruit and nuts spilling out of the cornucopia and attach to side of candle with large pins.

Decorating Ideas for Special Occasions

Once you gain the reputation of being a first-class candle maker you undoubtedly will be called upon by your friends to create special candles for special occasions such as commemorative wedding, anniversary or birthday candles. By commemorative wedding candles, we are referring to a candle or candles created from the remnants of the wedding tapers which are usually lit on each wedding anniversary. To the newly weds such a candle is priceless and will increase in sentimental value as the years roll by. Thus, when called upon to create such special candles it would be helpful to have a few ideas in mind to "draw from," for being asked to create a special-occasion candle on the spur of the moment can present a problem.

The ideas offered here should ease any confusion for each has been used successfully by some hobbyist in a similar situation.

COMMEMORATIVE WEDDING CANDLES

What could be a more meaningful gift for the newly weds than a beautiful candle created from the remnants of their wedding candles. It would remain in their home as a constant reminder of their wedding, their love and the vows they made . . . and on each anniversary, they could light the candle together in a simple traditional ceremony denoting their continued love and devotion toward one another. Candlelight has always meant warmth, friendliness, cheerfulness and romance; would there ever be a more appropriate time for soft candlelight than on a couple's wedding anniversary. Particularly when the candle contains the very candles which glowed warmly during their wedding ceremony.

Below are a few ideas for creating and decorating a commemorative wedding candle. Regardless of whether you decorate the candle or not, however, you may be assured that it will be a most cherished gift by its recipients.

Submitted by Mrs. Ethel Black (See Figure 178). Using the wax from the wedding candles fashion a large round or square candle. Apply whipped wax around the upper portion of the candle resembling a ribbon complete with bow. From the bow hang two or three white, frosted miniature bells.

Wedding picture candle (See Figure 179). Pour the wax from the melted-down remnants of the wedding candles into a large round, oval or square mold. Pin the newspaper picture of the newly weds onto the resulting candle with pearl headed pins or sequins and pins. Tie a silver or white ribbon around the candle with the bow situated just below the picture. Hang four or five miniature bells from the center of the bow.

Submitted by Bernice Kellis (See Figure 180). Create either a large round or square candle from the wedding candles and affix around its base a piece of ribbon and/or lace from the wedding bouquet. Stud the candle with half rhinestones, securing them with a dab of glue on their back side.

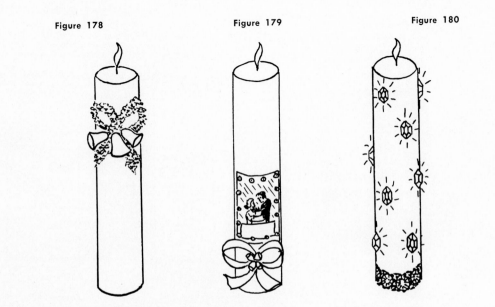

Figure 178   Figure 179   Figure 180

Wedding cake candle. Pour any large block candle and insert it into a six-inch square piece of styrofoam, positioning it so that a "platform" extends out in front of the candle. Stand the figures of the bride and groom from the wedding cake on this styrofoam platform and secure with whipped wax. The candle itself may be decorated with sequins, rhinestones, etc., or left plain.

ANNIVERSARY CANDLES

Golden anniversary (See Picture 93). Pour a white 3″ round candle. Stick mylar emblems "50" on one side framing the numerals with the outside portion of a gold medallion. Pin a gold border strip or gold metallic tape about the candle base.

Golden anniversary. Submitted by Mrs. Ethel Black (See Figure 181). Pour a white 3″ round candle. Affix a row of medallions about the base and small gold bells around the top using the small triangular spacers between the medallions from which to "hang" the bells. Pin the numeral "50" on the candle out of gold sequins.

Silver anniversary. Submitted by Mrs. C. C. Alexander of New Orleans, Louisiana (See Figure 182). Pour a white square hurricane candle. Fasten five or six miniature frosted white bells to two foil lovebirds. Attach the two birds to the candle with a sequin pin through the twisted wire at the top of the bells, thus leaving the birds slightly mobile. On the other side, attach numerals "25," using either mylar emblems or cardboard numerals sprayed silver.

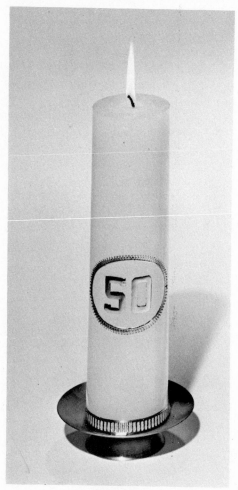

Picture 93

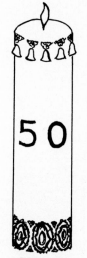

Figure 181

Figure 182

Silver anniversary. Secure a tall round white candle to a styrofoam base. Apply either silver or gold decorations depending on the occasion. Prepare a money plant by cleaning and removing all excess fiber. Spray the money plant with silver or gold metallic paint and push it into the styrofoam base in back of the candle. Insert silver or gold spikes into styrofoam base at the front and wire white bells into large bows of silver or gold lavalon lace and secure into the styrofoam about the base of the candle. Artificial white orange blossoms and leaves are pinned to the side of the candle, or if you prefer, attach silver or gold "25" or "50" to denote the anniversary year. The styrofoam base is "finished off" with a piece of silver or gold metallic tape pinned around the edge (See Group Picture II, Page 80b).

BIRTHDAY CANDLES

Submitted by Mrs. Ethel Black (See Figure 183). Pour a pale blue or pink square hurricane candle. Print a "Happy Birthday" message on one side and the age on the other side using glitter and glitter cement technique or a tube of **Glitter Magic or** similar type premixed tube glitter. Pin a gold border strip around the top and bottom of the shell to provide the finishing touch.

Clown face No. 1. Submitted by Mrs. Wm. R. Garvin of Vashon, Washington (See Figure 184). Pour a white cone candle. Cut out features of the clown's face, ears included, from colored beeswax sheets and pin onto candle. Apply a dab of whipped wax at the very top to resemble a pompon on the hat.

Figure 183

Figure 184

Clown face No. 2 (See Picture 94). Pour yellow wax into a large cone mold until it is half filled and let set for approximately two hours. Fill the remainder of the mold with white wax. Draw a symmetrical clown face on a piece of paper. Using your drawing as a pattern, pin prick the features onto the white portion of the candle and paint the features with colorful wax paint. Cover the dividing line between the yellow and white wax by creating a "hat brim" of some sort. The clown pictured has a rolled strip of sheet beeswax, but two alternate "brims" could be a thin strip of wax applied while warm and pliable—or a band of whipped wax.

Birthday decal candle (See Picture 95). Pour a tall round or tapered round white candle. Apply a birthday decal (available from Pourette Mfg.). This candle is a traditional birthday candle in that each birthday the celebrant burns the candle down to the number depicting his age.

Picture 94

Picture 95

MISCELLANEOUS NOVELTY CANDLES

Mardi Gras special. Submitted by Mrs. C. C. Alexander (See Figure 185). Pour a tan, round hurricane. Mold a brown mask from a plastic mold (purchased from a ceramics hobby shop). Attach the mask to the hurricane with melted wax or wax weld. Set candle on round hurricane base.

Figure 185

Ice cube candle (See Picture 96). Insert a slim tapered candle upside down into a 3″ round mold so that the wick from the taper extends through the wick hole at the mold base. Press a layer of mold sealer over the extending wick outside the mold base to protect it well from water. Dribble melted wax down the side of the upright taper until a thickness of wax approximately ¼″ is attained at the bottom of the mold. Allow this layer of wax to set for about 10 minutes, thus, concealing any exposed wick inside the mold. Drop small ice-cubes directly into the mold until the mold is completely filled. Pour wax at approximately 240° onto the ice cubes until all cubes are covered. Insert the mold into a warm water bath for the initial cooling period as is the normal procedure for most block candles. When wax has hardened, drain out the water and remove candle from the mold. Be sure to wipe mold dry of excess water to prevent rusting.

Picture 96

The irregular holes extending into the candle may be either left void or the candle may be repositioned in the mold and a harmonizing color of wax poured into the cavities, thus making a two-tone solid candle.

Hammered copper candle (See Picture 96-A). Make a round or oval block candle. Hit the candle surface with the round part of a ball-peen hammer forming small round indentations. If you don't have such a hammer, any small round object such as a marble, ball bearing, etc. held against the candle surface and then struck with a hammer will produce the same effect. Spray the entire candle copper or bronze.

Tree trunk candle (See Picture 97 and Group Picture I, Page 80a). Pour a tall 2″ or 3″ round brown candle. Cut 2″ lengths of wire from a coat hanger and bend them in irregular shapes to resemble broken tree limbs. Hold each piece of wire on a burner plate with pliers until hot; then press each one into the side of the candle, holding each piece steady until the wax around the wire cools. Apply brown whipped wax over entire candle, including wire "branches." If desired, you may smooth over the whipped wax surface by submerging candle in very hot water and rubbing down the rough spots. Entire candle may also be sprayed gold if desired. Stick small birds on a few of the branches for added realism. A hollow tree stump may be made the same way using a round hurricane mold and leaving the branches off.

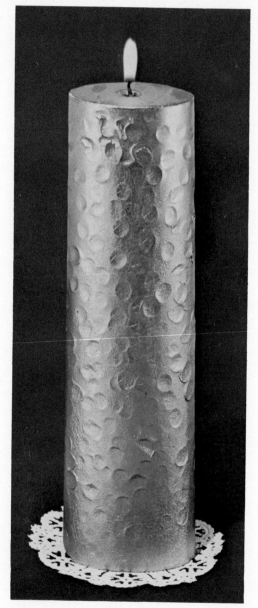

Picture 96-A

Picture 97

Beeswax hurricane candle. Submitted by Mrs. F. A. Hofer of Bluffton, Ohio (See Figure 186). Wrap a sheet of beeswax around any cylindrical shape with a diameter of at least 4″; mark overlapping section; remove from cylinder and trim off excess wax. Press the joining edges together, thus, forming an open cylinder. Set in styrofoam base and decorate around base with artificial flowers. As an alternate to beeswax you could wrap a thin layer of wax (formed in a large cookie sheet) around the cylinder.

Dice candle (See Picture 98). Procure any large square mold over three inches across. Measure the exact width of the mold and pour into the mold an equal depth of wax to obtain a true square form. Make a hollow wax shell by following the procedure used in creating a hurricane candle. Remove the wax shell from mold and drill holes to resemble the dots on dice. This entire procedure is fully explained under Filigree candles. After repositioning the red shell with the "dice holes" in the mold, suspend wick using the weighted wick method. Pour white wax (mixed with either stearic acid or luster crystals to obtain a pure white) into the red shell to within ½″ of its upper edge. When the white interior wax has completely set, pour a layer of red wax over the top to complete the sixth side of your dice.

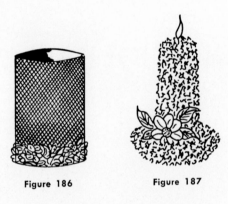

| Figure 186 | Figure 187 |

Combination block and hurricane candle. Fill a 3″ round mold with hard wax; let cool until the sides are set; pour out liquid wax from center. Refill interior with a lower melting temperature wax. When lit, the interior wax melts down while the harder exterior wax remains, leaving a thin shell through which the candle glows.

Wax candle and adjoining holder. Submitted by Mrs. Joseph Lapka of Solon, Ohio (See Figure 187). Pour a candle from a juice glass and a wax base from a sauce dish. Set the candle on the wax base and apply whipped wax to the entire surface except for the topside of the base. Glaze in hot wax bath and touch up with gold paint. Add seasonal decorations around base such as flowers, holly and berries, sea shells, etc.

Picture 98

PART V

IMPROVISED CANDLE HOLDERS AND BASES

Whether you intend to make an elaborate arrangement or merely construct a simple base for your candle, styrofoam is by far the easiest and simplest material with which to work. The "foam" comes in all shapes and sizes. Generally for a candle-holder or arrangement, however, a 6" round or square block, one or two inches thick, is suitable. Its popularity among candle hobbyists is certainly understandable: it can be easily carved into any shape; decorations such as boughs and artificial flowers can be stuck into it; any shaped candle can be set in it; and the same piece can be used over and over for different arrangements.

Mrs. G. A. Culpepper puts styrofoam to work throughout the year. She explains: "I cover a styrofoam base with pine boughs or holly at Christmas; moss for spring; colored leaves for fall. Also, for Christmas, I push stemmed Christmas balls into the foam and cluster around the base of the candle."

But we're getting ahead of ourselves. Let's first look into how styrofoam is used for candle arrangements. When used as a base, imbed the candle into the foam about ½" to 1" for added stableness. This is accomplished the following way:

Place the candle on the foam block and outline around the candle with a pencil.

Trace along the line with a knife, cutting into the block the desired depth.

"Scoop out" the center of the outlined figure by cutting out small sections at a time until the desired depth has been achieved.

Before setting the candle into position, pour a small amount of melted wax into the hole. When hard, this wax will provide the necessary rigidity to the upright candle.

The decorative items that can be affixed to the styrofoam are infinite. Stiff, pointed accessories, such as boughs, can be shoved directly into it while the more delicate stemmed articles, such as cattails, wheat and sea-oats can be inserted in preformed holes. Stemmed artificial fruit, nuts, bells and balls are pinned or stapled to the foam, while solid articles such as sea shells or stones are glued on.

Mrs. C. E. Crooks of Guthrie, Oklahoma, sent us Picture 99, illustrating how she used styrofoam and boughs to show off three tall, tapered white candles.

"The three candles were surrounded by magnolia leaves (sprayed gold) and sprigs of pine," she explained.

Picture 99

Perhaps the most appealing candle bases are those created from dried materials (cones, pods, nuts). These materials lend themselves exceptionally well to a candle display.

Mrs. Delbert Adamson of Hays, Kansas, writes: "My husband and I went out in the country and gathered pods and weeds. I sprayed them bronze, using a piece of styrofoam for a base in which to stick the sprayed weeds. I then made a deep yellow pyramid candle to sit on one side of the styrofoam; bought a small stuffed pheasant to place in front of the setting. This was all very simple and drew many compliments."

Mrs. Raymond DeBriar suggests yet another method of creating a candle base of cones and pods: "I cut an 8" circle of ¼" hardware cloth (wire mesh) and placed a holder, the size of the candle to be used, in the center. I had a special holder made that I wired to the center of the hardware cloth circle. Around the holder, I completely

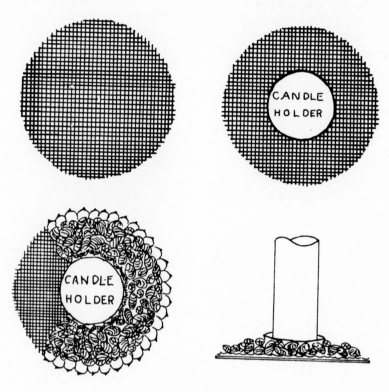

Figure 187-A

filled the rest of the circle with cones and pods from 2″ in size and down. I sprayed the cones lightly with gold and added miniature fruit for color. To firm the base, I drilled holes in an 8″ circle of masonite and wired it to the wire mesh on which the cones are wired. The candle then is placed in the holder" (See Figure 187-A).

If you have a wooden base for your candle, but aren't sure how to attach a candle to it, follow the advice of Mrs. Robert Kamrath:

"Pound three nails through the bottom side so the ends protrude out the top. Press points lightly on the candle base; heat a metal rod and insert rods into nail marks. The three holes in the candle base should then line up with the protruding nails; thus, when joined, giving stability to the candle."

Here's another idea for a home-made wooden holder as suggested by Mrs. Leslie Townsend: "Cut out a round circle of plywood and attach a 'thin wall holder' (purchased at any hardware or electrical store) for a handle; drive a nail through the bottom center to hold the candle and spray on paint. Glitter may also be applied" (See Figure 188).

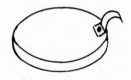

Figure 188

A "heritage wreath" created on a plywood base makes a very attractive candle base. Cones are normally attached to a circular plywood form by drilling a number of small holes through the form and tying the decorations on with wire. The wire ends are twisted together in back of the form, thus, holding the decorations firmly in place. Picture 99-A shows the results of gathering, assembling and securing a variety of nuts, cones, pods, etc. to a circular plywood form. Such a base, of course, may be used for years and enables you to create and use plain candles without the need of further decorating on the candle itself.

A popular hurricane base holder is one you merely glue together. Here's how: Glue four 1″ wooden balls on a piece of 6″ square ¾″ plywood, securing one ball at each corner. When the glue sets, paint it any desired color and your base is complete and ready for use. A round hurricane base is made similarly out of a round piece of plywood with three balls attached.

An 8-inch aluminum pie pan, a toy pie pan and a tuna fish can combine to make an attractive king-size candlestick for a bayberry candle (See Picture 100). Use a 3/16″ bolt 3″ long to bolt the three pieces together, with the can in the middle. Bolt on a 1″ conduit hanger for a handle. Give holder three coats of white enamel.

With a little extra push of imagination you can devise unique holders using odds and ends found in your home. As an example, for a Christmas tree base you can use a custard cup or painted spool. And if you have access to the sea shore, try this one: Set your candle in a sea shell, pour in wax to secure it, and stick on small shells, sand and glitter as the wax softens.

Picture 99-A

Picture 100—Bayberry candle and improvised holder

Mrs. Hazel Clampitt of St. Paul, Minnesota, certainly put her imagination to use in devising a holder made of wax. She writes: "Simply pour the same colored wax (less than 1″ deep) into a 5″ salad bowl. Then set a candle exactly in the middle and let stand until solid. After removing from the mold, decorate the base the same as the candle."

Here's another idea from Mrs. Clampitt, this one telling how to make a base for multi-colored or marbleized candles: "Use a one-pound coffee can for a mold. In the bottom center, set an inverted 3″ ash tray and fill in clear glow wax, enough to cover the ash tray about ½″. Then carefully add chunks of colored wax, pressing them under the melted wax. To unmold, simply cut the bottom out of the can and remove the ash tray. In the hollow made by the ash tray, pour a bit of melted wax and put in the chunk candle."

Mrs. Corinne Cook has improved a base which is not only attractive but functional and easy to create as well. "First, cut out a piece of cardboard the shape you wish your base to be," she instructs. "Mix up some plaster of paris and spread it over the cardboard, making 'hills and valleys' or any formation you wish. To avoid a mess, place the cardboard on a piece of wax paper prior to the application of the plaster. While the plaster is wet, imbed your candle into it and any decorating accessory you may desire at the base of the candle. You may also pour a coating of colorful wax over the plaster or sprinkle it with glitter for added color."

It is easy to understand the advantages of this base. It can be used for any size or shape of candle, decorations may be firmly affixed to it, and you can use it over and over again; just replace the candle when it burns down.

Mrs. Joseph Lapka of Solon, Ohio, merely uses a wire as a foundation for one of her bases.

"During the holiday season, I make wreaths on a single wire frame to set any of the large candles in. Some of these wreaths are made of various sized pine cones, green-brown velvet leaves and small colorful artificial fruit. Another wreath is made of artificial orange blossoms, leaves and small artificial oranges."

Mary Pruden offers excellent advice to those wishing to improvise a candle holder: "The bargain bin of the dime store china and glass counter are an unending source of odd saucers and dishes to stand your candles in."

A particularly striking arrangement for your mantel this Christmas would be to gild inexpensive goblets from the dime store with spray paint (See Figure 189). After paint

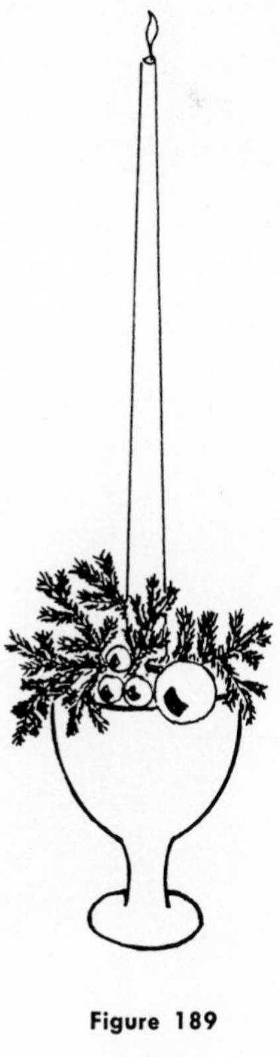

Figure 189

has dried thoroughly, tall tapers are placed securely in goblets by dropping a few spots of candle wax in bottom. Evergreen clippings from the Christmas tree are flanked around candles. Red Christmas balls in assorted sizes are fastened onto greens with tree-ornament hooks.

Many glasses or footed glass dishes make ideal holders when turned upside down. Mrs. Ernest Ohrstrom of Solon, Ohio, says that one of her favorites is a milk glass-footed cake plate. "I turn this upside down and place the candle in the stem. The base may be decorated with several supplemental decorations, such as artificial fruit, fresh flowers and greens, Christmas ornaments and holly."

Lawrence Rowland of Wichita, Kansas, uses sherbet glasses set upside down to hold tapers. "Place a bit of clay in the stem to steady the candlestick and decorate the body of the glass with Rineglas transfers and gold splatter paint."

An easy, yet stunning candle holder is an auto hubcap sprayed gold (See Picture 101). After the candle is inserted, encircle it with cones and greens.

Picture 101

PART VI

ROLLING BEESWAX CANDLES

The intent of this section is merely to introduce a simple but very popular method of making candles. No attempt will be made to explore the countless possibilities and innovations in using wax sheets. Such an exploration would fill volumes. We will merely describe and illustrate the simpler forms of hand-rolled candle shapes requiring no special artistic ability. Through experience and imagination, however, you will find yourself designing and creating innumerable decorative forms and having a wonderful time doing it.

There are various grades of beeswax sheets available, ranging from those composed of 100% pure beeswax to sheets composed of a wax blend consisting of a small portion of beeswax. We mention this for two reasons: (1) the pure beeswax sheets remain pliable at room temperature, making them easy to work with, while the blended wax sheets are vulnerable to breakage while shaping; (2) the pure sheets burn slower. Pure beeswax sheets can always be evidenced by their scent of honey.

Most sheets are 8″ wide by 16½″ long and have a honeycombed surface. The sheets may be rolled as they are—cut and rolled—or combined with other sheets and rolled, depending on the size of the candle you desire. In other words, the height, diameter and shape of the finished candle is determined solely by the size and shape of the sheet itself. Large-diameter candles may be made by rolling multiple sheets of beeswax together. Merely butt them, end to end, and keep on rolling.

Regardless of the candle-size or shape, the wick is always positioned in the same manner. When you are satisfied that the sheet is pliable enough to bend and roll without cracking—and it should be if at room temperature—position the sheet on a table with the length of the candle lying parallel with and extending about ¼″ beyond the table's edge. Press this overhanging portion down against the side of the table top, forming a slot into which the wick is placed (See Fig. 190-A). Flip the sheet over, lay the wick in

the fold and press the wick over the wax at intervals, keeping the wick taut at all times (See Fig. 190-B). When the wick has been completely sealed within the edge, continue rolling the sheet forward until the entire sheet has become rolled around the wick. Presto, you have a candle (See Fig. 190-C).

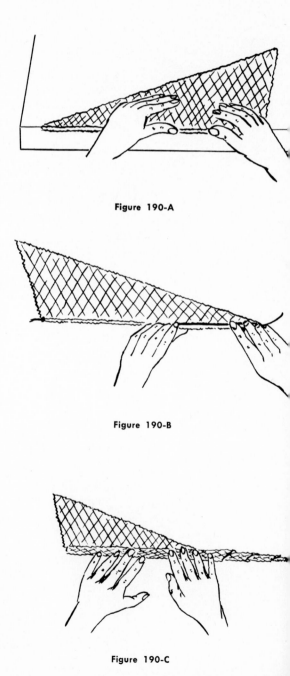

Figure 190-A

Figure 190-B

Figure 190-C

We believe in the old adage that "a picture is worth a thousand words," so rather than try to explain the basic sizes and shapes of the beeswax candles, we have illustrated them for you. Each illustration shows the size of the original sheet, how the sheet is cut, the direction of the roll and the size and shape of the completed candle. Incidentally, when cutting the sheets, place a straight edge, such as a ruler, along the line you want cut and draw a knife along the edge, cutting the wax as you go (See Figure 191).

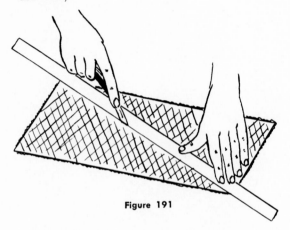

Figure 191

On the tapers, the trailing edge of the candle may be flared out, all the way around, providing added beauty to your creation (See Figure 192).

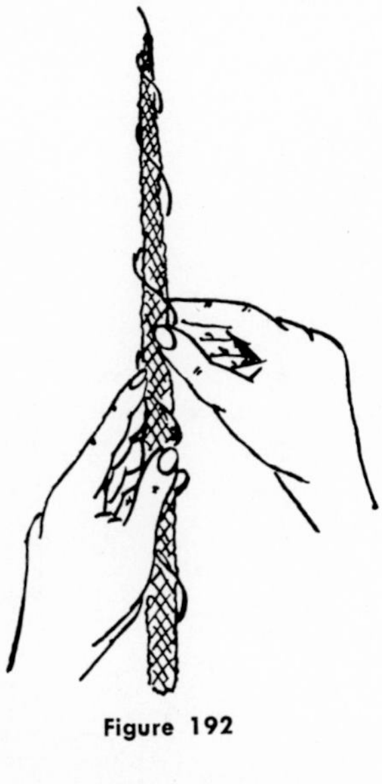

Figure 192

Picture 102 demonstrates four simple beeswax candles placed in driftwood candle holders; rolled from two sheets of beeswax (See Figure 202).

Picture 102

A variety of six beeswax candles are displayed in Picture 103, each candle a popular number for use in arrangements or wherever there's a need for a simple yet attractive beeswax candle.

From left to right, each candle is explained in the following figures:

Figure 200—using two different-colored sheets.

Figure 207—using four different-colored sheets.

Figure 195-B—decorated with green sequin leaves and holly berry pins.

Figure 193-B—with beeswax discs pressed on.

Figure 201—decorated with sequins.

Figure 204—with the trailing edges flared out.

Picture 103

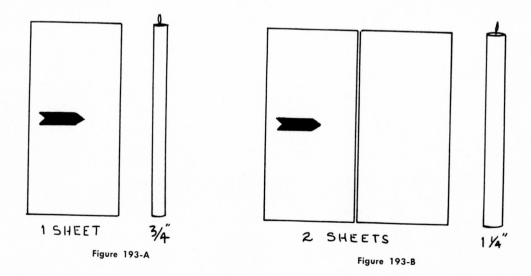

1 SHEET   3/4"

Figure 193-A

2 SHEETS   1¼"

Figure 193-B

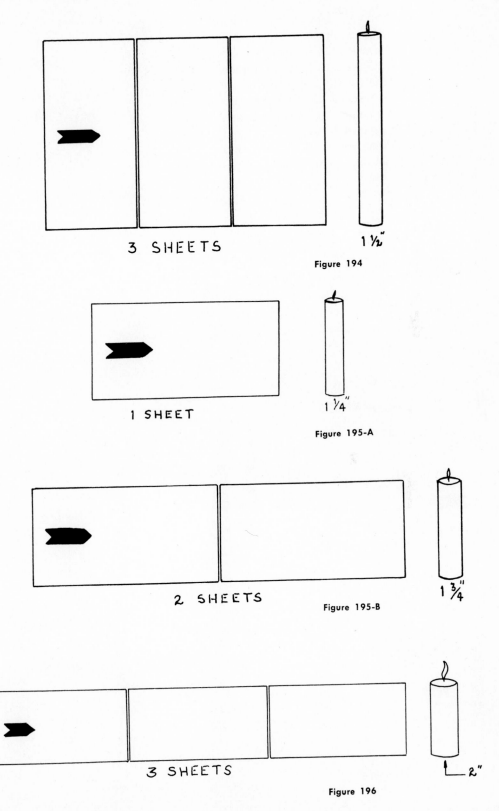

3 SHEETS   1 ½"

Figure 194

1 SHEET   1 ¼"

Figure 195-A

2 SHEETS   **Figure 195-B**   1 ¾"

3 SHEETS   2"

Figure 196

An example of how a beeswax candle can be shaped to form an unusual centerpiece is shown in Picture 104. Here a tall candle was rolled (See Figure 193-B). With thumb and forefinger, the candle was squeezed on alternating sides, forming round shallow indentations. These hollows can be left as are, but if color is preferred cut or stamp out small round discs from another colored sheet of beeswax and press them into the indentations.

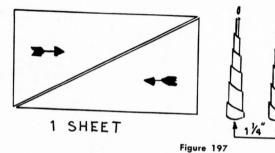

1 SHEET

Figure 197

DARKER COLOR

DIRECTLY UNDERNEATH

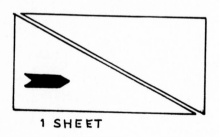

1 SHEET

Figure 198

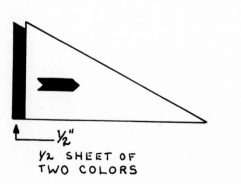

½ SHEET OF
TWO COLORS

Figure 199

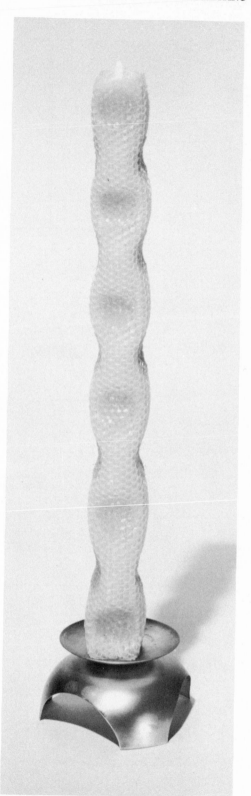

Picture 104

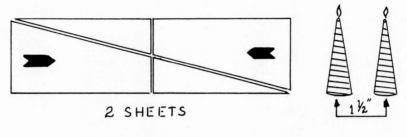

2 SHEETS

Figure 200

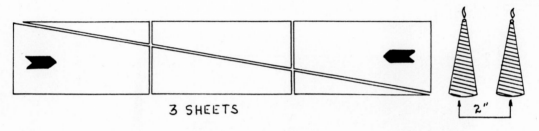

3 SHEETS

Figure 201

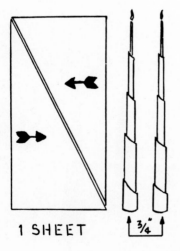

1 SHEET

Figure 202

DARKER COLOR
DIRECTLY UNDERNEATH

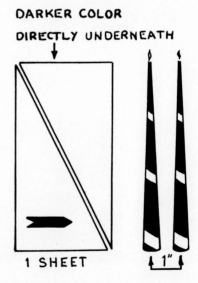

1 SHEET

Figure 203

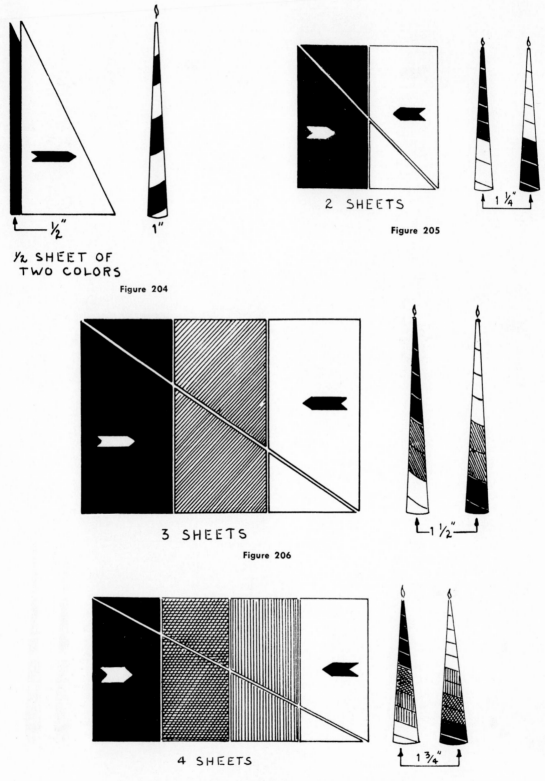

½ SHEET OF
TWO COLORS

Figure 204

2 SHEETS

Figure 205

3 SHEETS

Figure 206

4 SHEETS

Figure 207

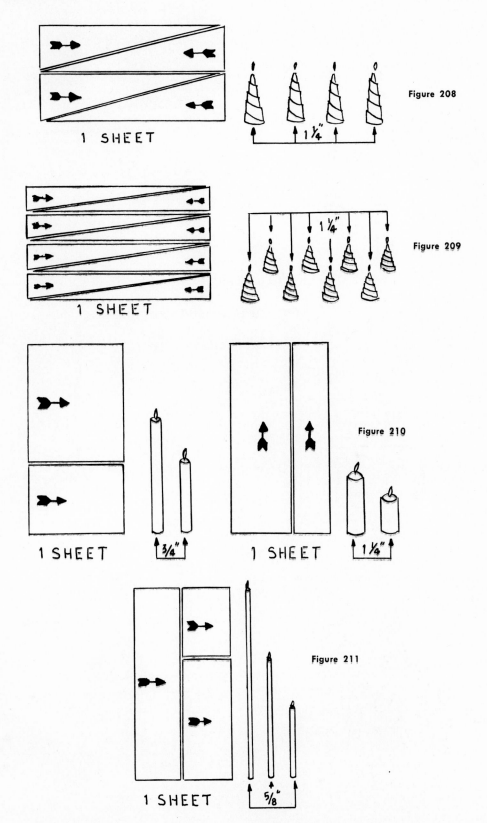

Figure 208

Figure 209

Figure 210

Figure 211

1 SHEET

1 SHEET

1 SHEET

1 SHEET

1 SHEET

We sincerely wish you

many enjoyable and satisfying

hours of candle-making.

Don Olsen   Ray D Cowie